In Memory
Dixie Kelly

1917 – 2002

About the Authors

Encouragement and inspiration for the compilation and publication of this new companion book for women's general household use was supplied by George's wife, Elizabeth, and Rex's wife, Dixie, which the authors affectionately acknowledge.

Spanish
for the
Housewife

by
George W. Kelly
Rex R. Kelly

ORDER FROM

KELLY BROTHERS
P.O. Box 210
Vanderpool, Texas 78885
(830) 966-3430

INTRODUCTION

The writers of Spanish for the Housewife were born near the Mexican border and have been closely associated throughout their lives with all classes of Mexicans. In their youth the writers learned the Spanish language as spoken along the border and in college took up Spanish as a major study. At this point they found that, although in all Latin American sections "Spanish is Spanish" with its basis in the Spanish of Spain, there are many and varied localisms of hard-to-trace origin in the language used in the United States, indeed, more such localisms than are found in the language of other countries.

They soon discovered that one who depends solely upon literary Spanish can scarcely converse with Mexicans of Mexico and areas of the U. S. because of the many slang expressions and localisms which have made this Spanish almost a separate language. The manner of talking which has grown up along the border might be called "Tex-Mex" meaning that many words of Mexican origin are half-Anglicized and have become fixed in the daily vocabulary of the border people. Since many Mexicans of the U. S. speak both languages, they have also taken many English words bodily and "espanolized" them. Then again, many of the words they use have been made without any thought of Spanish foundation, but rather for the purpose of realistic description.

Educated, cultured Mexicans from the cities of the interior do not themselves know many of the expressions in common usage in this country. There are, of course, expressions peculiar to certain areas of all large countries; but they seem few in number and easy to understand when compared with the language differences of urban Mexico and the border country.

In submitting this text the writers make no claim to a complete and exhaustive study of the subject. They have, however, reported the observations resulting from many years of close contact with Mexicans. In addition they have made a recent intensive investigation of Spanish for the Housewife as it is being used today. By these means they have enlarged as far as possible the list of words, phrases, and idioms which might have application to the home. It is in this way that they hope to make a contribution to the language for people preparing themselves for household duties. Many of the terms included are in use all over Mexico and the United States; some, only in one locality.

In making this study the authors have been unable to find the origin of some words; therefore, they have given both their Spanish and English meanings. They have found that the basis for many of the words are terms used in the United States. The Mexicans have coined many words for specific household purposes. Hence, there can be no bibliography for this text. The only bibliography is the Mexican people themselves, Mexicans of all classes.

PREFACE

Our purpose in compiling this book is to assist in the everyday activities of homes, many of which employ Spanish-speaking people part or all of the time. A working knowledge of Spanish will save much time and get better results on the job. We believe that this handy reference will be a great help toward those ends.

The first section of the book gives most of the things you will want to say in connection with ordinary housework. A separate chapter is devoted to each of the various types of housework such as setting the table, cleaning the bathroom, cleaning the kitchen, etc. When you are ready to do that particular job, turn to the chapter on that subject and start to work.

The second section gives some explanation of a few rules of grammar. Many of you will not be interested in this at all. You want to know what to say to get your work done and not why a word is used or how a sentence is made up. We believe, however, that some readers will be interested in the why and how of sentence formation. The basic rules of grammar will enable you to broaden your knowledge of Spanish much faster.

The last part of the book gives a list of commonly used English words arranged alphabetically with their Spanish equivalents and then Spanish words and their English equivalents.

Table of Contents

Subject Pronouns
Cardinal Numerals
Ordinal Numerals
Time Expressions
   Months of the Year
   Days of the Week
   Seasons of the Year
Present Tense
Possessive Adjectives
Direct Object Pronouns
Prepositional Pronouns
Past (preterite) Tense
Future Tense
Demonstrative Adjectives
Command Forms of Verbs
Indirect Object Pronouns
Gender of Nouns
The Definite Articles
Gender and Number of Adjectives
Possession of Nouns
Special use of "tener" and "hacer"
Other Expressions
Use of "ser" and "estar"
Present Participle
Accentuation
"It" as a Subject
Irregular Verbs

CHAPTER I

PRONUNCIATION

Pronunciation in Spanish is much simpler than in English. The letters a, e, i, o, and u are called vowels.

A   is always pronounced like the "a" in mama.

casa - pasa - habla

E   is pronounced like the long "a" in mate.

mesa - te - peso

In a syllable that ends in a consonant it is pronounced like the "e" in let.

es - del - este - tengo

I   is pronounced like the "ee" in meet.

si - piso - mi

O   is the same as the long "o" in so.

solo - tomo - todo

U   is pronounced like the "oo" in boot.

su - pluma - usted

The other letters are called consonants.

B   B and V are pronounced alike in Spanish and have the same sound. At the beginning of a word and after the letters "m" and "n" they are pronounced like the "b" in book.

1

bonito - bajo - ambos

At all other times the B and V are pronounced like the "v" in level.

beber - hablar - libro

C   is like K in English except when followed by an "e" or "i" and then it has the sound of "s".

como - casa - cinco

Ch   is considered a single letter of the Spanish alphabet and is pronounced like the "ch" in Church.

mucho - chico - muchacho

D   is like the English "d" except between vowels it sounds like the "th" in they.

dar - donde - lado

F   this letter is pronounced about the same as in English.

faltar - freno - fuego

G   is the same as in English except when followed by an "e" or "i" and then it is like an "h" in English.

pago - coger - gato

H   is always silent in Spanish.

hijo - hora - hoy

J   is always like the "h" in English.

hijo - frijole - méjico

K   there is no K in Spanish.

L   is pronounced about the same as in English.

    leche - lado - libre

LL   is considered a single letter in the Spanish alphabet and it is like a "y" in English.

    lleno - caballo - llevar

N   is approximately as in English.

    nada - noche - niño

Ñ   is like "ny" in English.

    mañana - año - leña

P   is approximately as in English.

    padre - poner - primo

Q   is like a "k" in English and is always followed by "u" which is silent.

    queso - quiero - que

R   is like the "r" in English but is slightly trilled in Spanish.

    rancho - rico - rojo

RR   is considered a single letter in the Spanish alphabet and is strongly trilled.

    perro - carro - cigarro

3

S   is pronounced about like the "s" in English.
     Before "d" and "m" it is more like a "z".

         solo - sacar - mismo

T   is approximately like the "t" in English.

         taza - todo - tiene

V   see explanation of B.

W   does not appear in Spanish.

X   has a "gs" sound when it is found between
     vowels.

         examen (eg-sa-men) - exacto

     When followed by a consonant it has an "s"
     sound. Many people do not make this dis-
     tinction and pronounce the "x" the same as
     in English.

         explicar - expreso - extensión

Y   standing alone means "and" and is pronounced
     like the English long "e".

         ley - rey - y

     As a consonant it is pronounced like the "y"
     in Yuma.

         yo - ayer - leyes

Z   is approximately like "s" in English.

         zero - tiza - zapato

4

ACCENTUATION

Words may be divided into parts or syllables. You generally raise your voice higher on one syllable than the others. This is called the accented syllable. Words ending in a vowel (a, e, i, o, u) or "n" or "s" are accented on the next to the last syllable; all others are accented on the last syllable, unless they have a written accent mark (').

casa	caballo	pasar
vamos	tractor	hablan
pase	algodón	frijole

CHAPTER II

GETTING ACQUAINTED NOS CONOCEMOS

Good morning, I am the lady of the house.	Buenos días, yo soy la ama de la casa (la patrona).
Have you done house work before?	¿Ha hecho Vd. los quehaceres de la casa antes?
Yes, for about six months.	Sí, por unos seis meses.
Have you worked as a maid before?	¿Ha trabajado Vd. de criada (servidora) antes?
No, but I have worked in my home.	No, pero he trabajado en mi casa.
Are you married?	¿Es casada?
No, I am single.	No, soy soltera.
How old are you?	¿Qué edad tiene? ¿(Cuántos años tiene?)
I am eighteen years old.	Tengo diez y ocho años.
Where do your parents live?	¿Dónde viven sus padres?
My father is dead; my mother lives in Monterrey.	Mi padre (papá) está muerto; mi madre (mamá) vive en Monterrey.
Do you have any brothers and sisters?	¿Tiene Vd. hermanos?

Yes, seven.	Sí, siete.
Where are they?	¿Dónde están?
They live with my mother.	Viven con mi mamá. (madre)
I want to show you the house.	Quiero enseñarle la casa.
There are three bedrooms, a living room, a family room, two baths, a kitchen, and a dining room.	Hay tres recámaras (alcobas), sala, ante-sala, dos cuartos de baño, una cocina, y un comedor.
This is the living room. We do not use it much.	Ésta es la sala. No la usamos mucho.
Here is the family room where we spend a lot of time.	Ésta es la ante-sala donde pasamos mucho tiempo.
This bedroom has a bath.	Esta recámara tiene un baño.
The other bathroom is between the other bedrooms.	El otro baño está entre medio las otras recámaras.
You will live in the little house in the back.	Vd. va a vivir en la casita de atrás.
It has everything you need.	Tiene todo que necesita.
You can eat here.	Puede comer aquí.

CHAPTER III

THE TABLE   LA MESA

I am going to show you how to set the table.	Voy a enseñarle poner la mesa.
The plates, silver, and glasses are placed on the table like this.	Se ponen los platos, la vajilla, y los vasos así (en esta manera).
Put the salt and pepper containers (shakers) and the sugar bowl on the table with each meal.	Ponga el salero, el pimentero, y el azúcar en la mesa con cada comida.
Take them off after each meal.	Quítelos despues de cada comida.
We use paper napkins most of the time.	Usamos servilletas de papel la mayor parte del tiempo.
I want to use the linen tablecloth today, and also the good china.	Quiero usar el mantel de lino hoy y también la loza (vasija) buena.
We will use place mats this time.	Usamos servilletas tapete esta vez.
There are four for lunch.	Somos cuatro para el almuerzo.
We have roast beef, salad, beans, squash, and cornbread.	Tenemos rosbif, ensalada, frijoles, calabaza, y pan de maíz.
Also iced tea and coffee to drink.	También, té helado y café para tomar.
While we are eating, stay near the door.	Mientras que comemos, quédese cerca de la puerta.

I will call you if I need anything.	Le llamo si necesito algo.
Bring some more bread.	Traiga mas pan.
The lady wants another cup of coffee.	La señora quiere otra taza de café.
We have finished; you can eat now.	Ya terminamos; Vd. puede comer ahora.
Then take everything from the table.	Entonces, quite todo de la mesa.
Use this brush to clean up the crumbs.	Use este cepillo para limpiar las migas.
Throw the scraps in the garbage can.	Eche las sobras en la basura.
You can wash the dishes in the dishwasher.	Puede lavar los trastos en la lavadora de trastes.
Before putting them in the machine, rinse them in warm water.	Antes de ponerlas en la máquina, enjuéguelos con agua tibia.
Put the plates on their edges like this.	Ponga los platos en sus bordes así.
The glasses go upside down on the pegs.	Los vasos van vueltos en las clavijas.
In order to start the machine, press (pull) this button.	Para comenzar la máquina, aprete (restire) este botón.
The machine stops itself.	La máquina se para solo.

CHAPTER IV

THE BATHROOM	EL BAÑO
I want to clean the bathroom everyday.	Quiero limpiar el baño todos los días.
Use this powder (soap) on the lavatory and tub.	Use este polvo (jabón) en la lavadora y el baño.
Clean with this brush. (rag)	Limpie con este cepillo. (trapo)
Change the towels every day.	Cambie las toallas todos los días.
Put the bath towels on this rack and the hand towels on the other one.	Ponga las toallas de baño en esta barra y las toallas de mano en la otra
The dirty towels go in the basket.	Las toallas sucias van en la cesta (canasta).
The clean towels and wash cloths (rags) are in this cabinet.	Las toallas y toallas jaboneras limpias están en este gabinete.
Clean the floor with this mop, warm water and soap.	Limpie el suelo con este trapeador, agua tibia y jabón.
Sometimes we don't use the other bathroom.	A veces no usamos el otro baño.
It is for our guests.	Es para nuestras huéspedes.
If nobody has used the bathroom, you need not clean it.	Si nadie ha usado el baño, no necesita limpiarlo.
If the door of the bathroom is closed, knock before entering.	Si la puerta del baño está cerrada, llame antes de entrar.

Spray glass cleaner on mirror, and doors of bath shower.	Eche este líquido en el espejo y las puertas de la ducha.
Wipe it good with dry cloth.	Séquelo bien con el trapo seco.
This is tile cleaner.	Éste es para limpiar teja.
Spray on, wipe with damp sponge, then dry with cloth.	Échelo, limpie con una esponja mojada, y entonces seque con un trapo.
Sprinkle this cleaner on inside of commode.	Salpique (eche) este líquido en el excusado.
Hang brush here to dry and put in closet on hook.	Ponga (colgue) el cepillo aquí para secar y entonces póngalo en el (camarín) en la clavija (colgadero).
Use wet sponge and cleanser for bath tub.	Use esponja mojada y líquido en el baño.
Dry tub with towel.	Seque el baño con toalla.
Mop linoleum every other day.	Limpie el linóleo cada dos días.
Put another roll of toilet paper in the bathroom.	Ponga otro rollo de papel para excusado en el baño.
There is a hanger near commode.	Hay una barra cerca del excusado.

11

CHAPTER V

THE BEDROOMS
LAS RECÁMMARAS

Dust the furniture with this rag.	Sacuda los muebles con este trapo.
Put a little furniture polish on the rag.	Ponga un poco de aceite en el trapo.
Use the vacuum cleaner on the rug.	Use el aspirador en la alfombra.
There are two electric outlets (plugs) in each room.	Hay dos enchufadores eléctricos en cada cuarto.
First plug in the cord.	Primero, conecte la cuerda.
We change the sheets and pillow cases twice a week.	Cambiamos las sábañas y fundas de almohada dos veces cada semana.
I will help you turn the mattress.	Yo le ayudo voltear el colchón.
Take the blankets off of the beds.	Tome (Quite) las frazada de las camas.
The clean bed linens are in the closet.	El lino limpio está en el gabinete.
Put fresh sheets and pillow cases on the beds.	Ponga sábeñas y almohadas limpias en las camas.
Move this night stand (lamp table) over near the head of the bed.	Mueva esta mesita cerca de la cabeza de la cama.

Put the chair on the other side of the bed.	Ponga la silla al otro lado de la cama.
This lamp stays on the little round table.	Ésta lámpara se queda en la mesita redonda.
Be careful not to break it.	Cuidado que no la quiebre.
Put the little one on the dressing table.	Ponga la chiquita en el tocador.
Leave the comb and brush on the dresser.	Deje el peine y el cepillo en el tocador.
The room looks nice.	El cuarto se ve bien.
Let's see if we can move this chest of drawers.	A ver si podemos mover esta cómode.
The shirts go in the large drawers.	Las camisas van en los cajones grandes.
Put the socks in the upper drawers.	Ponga los calcetines en los cajones de arriba.
Leave the underwear out.	Deje afuera la ropa interior.
Take it to the other bedroom.	Llévela a la otra recámera.
Separate the large from the small.	Separe lo grande de lo pequeño. (chico)

CHAPTER VI

THE KITCHEN   LA COCINA

Do you know how to cook?	¿Sabe Vd. cocinar?
Yes, I cook at my home.	Sí, cocino en mi casa.
When I am here, I will do most of the cooking.	Cuando estoy aquí, yo hago la mayor parte de la cocer.
I work five days a week, but I do not work on Saturday or Sunday.	Trabajo cinco días por semana, pero no trabajo el sábado o el domingo.
I want you to prepare breakfast today.	Quiero que Vd. prepare el desayuno hoy. (almuerzo)
My husband wants two fried eggs, two pieces of buttered toast, two pieces of bacon (ham), and coffee.	Mi esposo quiere dos huevos fritos, dos pedazos de pan tostado con mantequilla, dos pedazos de tocino (jamón), y café.
I want only toast and coffee.	Quiero no mas pan tostada y café.
Don't turn the eggs over.	No voltee los huevos.
Tomorrow, we will eat scrambled eggs and sausage.	Mañana, comemos huevos revueltos y chorizo.
I want a small glass of orange juice also.	Quiero un vasito de jugo de naranja también.
Bring the jar of jelly and the butter.	Traiga el vaso de jalea y la mantequilla.

14

Wash all fresh fruit real good.	Lave bien toda la fruta fresca
Wash celery and lettuce this way.	Lave acelga y lechuga así.
You make iced tea as I show you.	Yo le enseño hacer el té helado.
Put plenty of ice in glasses.	Ponga bastante hielo en los vasos.
Slice a lemon and put on table.	Corte un limón en pedazos y ponga en la mesa.
Sprinkle this dressing on salad and mix well.	Salpique (eche) esta salsa en la ensalada y mezcle bien.
These things must not go in dishwasher.	Estas cosas no van en el lavaplatos.
You must wash anything with wooden handles.	Debe lavar por mano las cosas con mango (palanca) de madera.
We use these dishes and silver every day.	Usamos esta vajilla (platos) y trastes todos los días.
Set the table with good silver and china.	Ponga la mesa con vasija y loza buena.
Wrap roast in foil and cook this temperature.	Envuelva la carne en este papel de estaño y use (cocine) esta temperatura.
After two hours unwrap foil a little while.	Después de dos horas desenvuelva por poco rato (unos minutos).

15

Another cup of coffee please.	Otra taza de café, por favor.
The coffee is cold; put it on the stove.	El café está frío; póngalo en la estufa.
Put a little shortening in the frying pan and use medium heat.	Pónga un poco de manteca en la cazuela y use calor mediano.
Get a package of meat out of the deep-freezer. (refrigerator)	Saque un paquete de carne del enfriadero (refrigerador).
Leave it out for three hours.	Déjelo afuera por tres horas.
Then put it in the oven.	Entonces, póngalo en el horno.
Use 400 degree heat for three hours.	Use calor de cuatro cientos grados por tres horas.
With the roast beef we will have green beans, cabbage, beets, and lettuce salad.	Con el rosbif (carne asada) tenemos ejotes, repollo, (col), betabeles, y ensalada de lechuga.
Where is the salad dressing?	¿Dónde está la salsa para ensalada?
Here it is in this bottle.	Aquí está en esta botella.
You can cut the meat with this electric knife.	Puede cortar la carne con este cuchillo eléctrico.
Put a little more salt on the cabbage.	Eche un poco mas sal en el repollo.
I like the beans, but they need a piece of pork.	Me gustan los frijoles, pero necesitan un pedazo de puerco.

16

CHAPTER VII

CLEANING THE WINDOWS	LIMPIANDO LAS VENTANAS

Today, we will clean the windows and screens.

Hoy, limpiamos las ventanas y los biombos tela.

First take off the screens.

Primero, quite los biombos.

Spray this liquid on the glass.

Eche este líquido en el vidrio.

You will have to use the step ladder.

Tiene que usar la escalera.

Be careful not to fall.

Tenga cuidado que no caiga.

Then wipe the glass with this cloth.

Entonces limpie el vidrio con este trapo.

Dry them well with this soft cloth.

Séquelas bien con esta tela suave.

Put them here against the wall.

Póngalas aquí contra la pared.

Brush the screens with this brush.

Cepille los telas biombos con este cepillo.

Now, wash them with water from the hose.

Ahora, lávelos con agua de la manguera.

Put them in the sun to dry.

Póngalos en el sol para secar.

Are they dry?

¿Están secos?

I think so.

Creo que sí.

Ok, put them back on.

Está bien, póngalos otra vez.

Are you tired?

¿Está Cansada?

Rest awhile.

Descanse un poco.

WASHING CLOTHES	LAVANDO LA ROPA
Pick up the dirty clothes.	Levante la ropa sucia.
Put it in the basket.	Póngala en esta canasta. (cesto)
Separate the white clothes from the colored.	Separe la ropa blanca de la de color.
Put a cup of washing powder on the clothes.	Ponga una taza de polvo para lavar en la ropa.
Pull this button to start the machine.	Estire este botón para comenzar la máquina.
When the machine stops, take the clothes out.	Cuando se para la máquina, saque la ropa.
Hang them on the line.	Cuélguelas en la linea. (tendedor)
The clothes pins are in this bag.	Las pinzas de tendedor están en este saco.
Are the clothes dry?	¿Está seca la ropa?
I will see.	Voy a ver.
No, they are still wet.	No, todavia son mojadas.
It is going to rain.	Va a llover.
Look at those black clouds.	Mire aquellas nubes negras.

I will get the clothes.	Yo levanto (recojo) la ropa.
There comes the rain. (water, and hail also)	Allá viene la lluvia. (agua y granizo también)
Close the windows.	Cierre las ventanas.
Fill washing machine to this point with clothes.	Llene la máquina de lavar hasta este punto con ropa.
Do not put too many clothes in the machine.	No ponga demasiada ropa en la máquina.
Put clothes in dryer and turn this knob.	Ponga la ropa en la secadora y toque este botón.
Hang these on coat hangers when machine goes off.	Cuando se apague la máquina, ponga estas en colgaderos.
They do not have to be ironed.	No necesita plancharlas.

CHAPTER IX

IRONING   EL PLANCHAR

On Mondays you can wash the clothes in the machine.	Los lunes Vd. puede lavar la ropa en la máquina.
I will show you how to fix the ironing board so that it will stand up.	Le enseño arreglar la tábla como se queda de pie.
The ironing board is in the closet.	La planchadora está en el gabinete.
Do you know how to iron?	¿Sabe Vd. planchar?
We don't iron many things here.	No planchamos muchas cosas aquí.
You should iron on Tuesday.	Debe planchar los martes.
But if you do not have time, it is allright the next day.	Pero si no tiene tiempo, está bien el día siguiente.
We take most of my dresses to the cleaners.	Llevamos la mayor parte de mis vestidos a la lavandería.
The tailorshop cleans and presses my husband's suits.	La sastrería limpia y plancha los trajes de mi esposo.
We don't iron socks, underwear and some of the slacks.	No planchamos los calcetines, ropa interior, y algunos de los pantalones.
Put a little starch on the shirts.	Ponga un poco del almidón en las camisas.
Iron these khaki trousers also.	Planche estos pantalones de kaki tambien.

20

This is spray starch for ironing.	Hay almidón para planchar.
Shake well, spray small amount on clothes and iron.	Sacuda bien, eche un poco en la ropa y planche.
This lever is temperature control of iron.	Esta palanca (mango) arregla la temperatura de la plancha.
Iron must be warm for these clothes.	La plancha tiene que estar caliente para esta ropa.
Turn temperature to hot for these clothes.	Cambie la temperatura a caliente para esta ropa.

CHAPTER X

THE BARBEQUE	LA BARBACOA
Today we are having a barbeque.	Hoy tenemos una barbacoa.
About fifteen people will come.	Vienen unos quince personas.
We will cook two cabritos.	Cocemos dos cabritos.
John is bringing the meat.	Juan trae la carne.
Put salt and pepper on both sides.	Ponga sal y pimiento en ambos lados.
The fire is ready.	La lumbre está lista.
Now we will make some barbeque sauce.	Ahora, hacemos salsa para barbacoa.
Use this pan on the stove.	Use esta olla en la estufa.
Put in a half pound of butter and a cup of lard.	Ponga media libra de mantequilla y una taza de manteca.
Use five tablespoons of salt two of pepper, one of onion powder, and a little garlic.	Use cinco cucharas de sal, dos de pimiento, uno de polvo de cebolla, y un poco de ajo.
When the butter is melted, add three bottles of ketchup, a cup of lemon juice, two tablespoons of sugar, a small bottle of worchestershire, a bottle of A - 1 sauce, and a little tabasco sauce.	Cuando está derretida la mantequilla añada tres botellas de salsa de tomate, una taza de jugo de limón, dos cucharas de azucar, una botella chica de worchestershire, una botella de salsa A-1 y un poco salsa tabasco.

22

Clean the two outside tables.	Limpie las dos mesas de afuera.
We will fix the beans, salad, and tea inside.	Preparamos los frijoles, la ensalada, y el té adentro.
Put the beans in this pot and fill with water.	Ponga los frijoles en esta olla y llene con agua.
Set the electric stove at 300 degrees.	Ponga la estufa eléctrica a tres cientos grados.
Next we will mix the salad.	Entonces mezclamos la ensalada.
Cut the lettuce, tomatoes, and avocados into small pieces.	Corte en pedazos chicos la lechuga, los tomates, y los avocados.
Put these three bottles of salad dressing on the table.	Ponga estas tres botellas de aceite de ensalada en la mesa.
When the meat is ready, take all the food outside to the long table.	Cuando está lista la carne, lleve toda la comida a la mesa larga afuera.
My husband will cut up the meat.	Mi esposo corta la carne.
We will use paper plates and cups.	Usamos platos y tazas de papel.
Put ten plates and ten cups on the table.	Ponga diez platos y diez tazas en la mesa.
Fill each cup with ice.	Llene cada taza con hielo.

Then fill each cup.	Entonces llene cada taza.
Cut up this lemon in small slices.	Corte este limón en pedacitos.
Put napkins, forks, knives, and spoons with each plate.	Ponga servilletas, cuchillos, tenedores y cucharas con cada plato.
Now you can serve the dinner.	Entonces Vd. puede servir la comida.
When we finish, throw the plates, cups and napkins in the trash.	Cuando acabamos, tire vd los platos, tazas y servilletas en la basura.
Then you may wash the other things.	Entonces vd puede lavar las otras cosas.

THE PETS	LOS SANCHOS
Here we have a dog, two cats and three birds.	Aquí tenemos un perro, dos gatos y tres pájaros.
Let the dog out of the pen every morning.	Déjele salir el perro del corral todas las mañanas.
Give him food from this can.	Déle comida de esta lata.
Let him in the house.	Déjele entrar la casa.
We will bathe the dog today.	Bañamos el perro hoy.
Bring the soap and hot water.	Traiga vd el jabón y agua caliente.
Wash him good with this brush.	Lávele bien con este cepillo.
Then dry him with this towel.	Entonces sequele con esta toalla.
Give the cats food once a day.	Dele comida a los gatos una vez al día.
Give the kittens milk every day.	Dele comida a los gatos vez al día.
Clean out the bird cage.	Limpie el cajón de pájaros.
Give them seed and water every day.	Delos semillas y agua cada día.
Don't let them out of the cages.	No los deje salir de los cajones.

CHAPTER XII

OTHER HOUSEHOLD DUTIES   OTROS QUEHACERES

Today you and your wife
may help Mrs. Wilson in
the house.

Hoy Vd. y su esposa pueden
ayudar la señora Wilson en
la casa.

First, you may sweep all
the house with the broom.

Primero, pueden barrer toda
la casa con la escoba.

With these rags clean all
the dust from the furniture.

Con estos trapos limpie todo
el polvo de los muebles.

Friday each week go over all
furniture with lemon oil.

Cada viernes limpie todo el
mueble con aceite de limón.

Use this cloth to put the
oil on furniture.

Use esta tela para poner el
aceite en el mueble.

After a few minutes polish
with this kind of dry
cloth.

Después de pocos minutos,
brille con esta clase de
tela seca.

There are plenty of dry
cloths.

Hay bastante telas secas.

The lemon oil and cloths
are kept here.

El aceite de limón y telas
se quedan aquí.

I will show you what to
clean with each attachment
of the vacuum cleaner.

Yo le enseño como se usa
cada aparato del aspirador.

The cloth bag is emptied
this way each week.

Se descarga el saco de tela
cada semana en esta manera.

This is how paper bags
go in portable vacuum
cleaner.

Se pone el saco del aspirador
portátil así.

Each week clean baseboards, doors and trim.	Cada semana limpie las tablas, puertas y bordos.
Dust first then wipe with damp sponge and dry.	Primero sacuda entonces limpie con esponja mojada y seque.
Spray this cleaner on baseboards, doors and trim.	Eche este líquido en las tablas, puertas, y bordos.
Wipe with a dry cloth.	Limpie con trapo seco.
Today I want the room paneling wiped off.	Hoy, limpie los entrepaños.
Do this once a month.	Haga esto una vez cada mes.
The refrigerator needs to be cleaned.	El refrigerador debe ser limpiado.
Put things from each shelf on cabinet.	Ponga las cosas de cada estante en el gabinete.
Use this amount of water and soda (soap) to clean it.	Use esta cantidad de sosa (jabón) y agua para limpiarlo.
Wipe with damp sponge and dry.	Limpie con esponja mojada y séquelo.
Clean inside of all cabinets today.	Limpie adentro todos gabinetes hoy.
Wipe cabinets with damp sponge and dry.	Limpie los gabinetes con esponja mojada y séquelos.

Clean one shelf at a time to keep things in order.	Limpie los estantes uno por uno para guardar todo en orden.
Watch me make cornbread and biscuit.	Vd. puede mirarme hacer pan de maís y bísquetes.
Write it down if you cannot remember.	Escríbalo si no puede recordar.
Broil two rare and two well done steaks.	Emparille dos biftecs crudos y dos bien cocidos.
We put the food in these bowls in the refrigerator.	Ponemos la comida en estas ollas en la enfriadera (refigerador).
This is polish to clean the silver.	Éste es el líquido para limpiar la vasija.
Put small amount on damp sponge and rub good.	Ponga un poco en esponja mojada y fregue bien.
Wash in soapy water, rinse good, and dry.	Lave con agua y jabón, enjuague, y seque.
Silver must be dried real good or it will have spots.	Hay que secar la vasija muy bien o se queda con manchas.
There are plenty of dry cloths in this drawer.	Hay bastante trapos (telas) secos en este cajón.
Clean the curtains, rug, and divan (sofa) with the vacuum cleaner.	Limpie las cortinas, la alfombra, y el diván (sofá) con el aspirador (vacuum).
Use this attachment on curtains and divan.	Use este aparato en las cortinas y el divan.

28

You need to sweep and mop the outside porch.	Necesita escobar y limpiar el portal con mop.
Wash sidewalk with a broom and water from the hose.	Lave la banqueta con escoba y agua de la manguera.
Clean bookcases today.	Limpie los armarios de libros hoy.
Stack books like this on the table.	Ponga los libros como éste en la mesa así.
Clean one shelf at a time.	Limpie no mas un estante a una vez.
The paint brush is good to get dust from books.	El cepillo (brochón) es bueno para limpiar el polvo de los libros.
Wipe books with cloth too.	Limpie los libros con trapo también.
Set the table this way.	Ponga la mesa en esta manera.
Put the flowers in middle of table.	Ponga las flores en medio de la mesa.
You offer food to guests on left side.	Sirva la comida a los huéspedes al lado izquierdo.
Serve first the lady sitting on the right of my husband.	Sirva primero la mujer sentada a la derecha de mi esposo.
Remove plates from left side of the person.	Levante (quite) los platos del lado izquierdo de la persona.

When serving food hold platter or bowl this way.	Cuando está sirviendo la comida, agarre el plato así.
Bring cream and sugar for coffee.	Traiga creme y azúcar para el café.
Keep glasses filled with water.	Los vasos deben estar lleno de agua todo el tiempo.
This pitcher is for the water.	Este jarro es para el agua.
Butter goes in this dish with knife.	La mantequilla va en este plato con este cuchillo.
Put cloth on plate and then the bread.	Ponga tela en el plato y entonces el pan.
Fold over cloth to keep bread warm.	Doble la tela en el pan y se queda caliente.

CHAPTER XIII

WE GO SHOPPING	VAMOS DE COMPRAS
Today, I am going down-town shopping.	Hoy, voy de compras al centro.
You can go with me.	Vd. puede ir conmigo.
Put this suit and dress in the car.	Ponga este traje y vestido en el carro.
I want to take them to the tailorshop.	Quiero llevarlos a la sastrería.
I also want to return this box of cereal.	Quiero devolver esta caja de cereal.
It is no good. It has weevils in it.	No sirve. Tiene gorgojos (animales).
Close the windows. It looks like it is going to rain.	Cierre las ventanas. Parece que va a llover.
Look at those dark clouds.	Mire aquellas nubes negras.
Leave the dog outside.	Deje afuera el perro.
Is the stove turned off?	¿Está apagada la estufa?
I will see.	Voy a ver.
Cut off the lights.	Apague las luces.
Are you ready?	¿Está lista?
Where is your coat?	¿Donde está su abrigo? (saco)

Bring your purse.	Traiga Vd. su bolsa.
It is a little cold. (chilly)	Hace poco frío.
Open the garage door.	Abre la puerta del garaje.
Leave it open.	Déjela abierta.
This is the cleaners.	Esta es la sastrería.
Take the clothes inside.	Lleve la ropa adentro.
Ask them when I can pick them up.	Pregúnteles cuando puedo levantarlas.
Tell them my name and address.	Dígales mi nombre y dirección.
What did they say?	¿Qué dijeron?
Day after tomorrow at five.	Pasado mañana a las cinco.
Wait for me here.	Espéreme aquí.
I want to buy a pack of cigarettes.	Quiero comprar un paquete de cigarros.
Let's go to the women's clothing store.	Vámonos a la tienda de ropa para damas. (mujeres)
There is a sale on there now.	Hay una barata (venta) allí ahora.
Sometimes there are some good bargains.	A veces hay unas buenas gangas.

Most of the time their dresses are high.	La mayor parte del tiempo sus vestidos son caros.
I want to buy you a dress.	Quiero comprarle un vestido.
Look at them and pick out one that you like.	Mírelos y escoja uno que le gusta.
What size do you wear?	¿Qué talle usa Vd.?
Do you like this one?	¿Le gusta éste?
It is wool.	Es de lana.
It is pretty.	Es bonito.
Try it on.	Pruébelo.
It looks a little tight.	Parece un poco apretado.
Let's see if they have a larger one.	A ver si tienen otro mas grande.
This one fits me well.	Éste me queda bien.
Good, I will buy it for you.	Bueno, se lo compro.
But Mrs. B., it costs twenty two dollars.	Pero Señora B., cuesta veinte y dos dólares.
That doesn't matter.	No importa.
Do you want a hat?	¿Quiere Vd. sombrero?
No, I use a scarf.	No, uso chalina.
I need two pair of panty hose.	Necesito dos pares de panti medias.

33

OK, what color?	¿Está bien, de que color?
What else do you need?	¿Qué mas necesita?
That's all.	Es todo.
Let's go to the drug store.	Vamos a la botica.
I want to buy a lipstick and some aspirin.	Quiero comprar un lápiz de labio (colorete) y unas aspirinas.
Do you need anything?	¿Necesita Vd. algo?
Yes, some rouge and shampoo.	Si, colorete y champú.
They have many brands of makeup here.	Tienen muchas marcas de maquillaji aquí.
Do you know what brand you want?	¿Sabe Vd. la marca que quiere?
No, but I know the color.	No, pero sé el color.
Now to the supermarket for groceries.	Ahora al super para abarrotes.
I have a list of some of the things.	Tengo una lista de algunas de las cosas.
I have to turn to the right here.	Tengo que dar vuelta a la derecha aquí.
Do you know how to drive?	¿Sabe Vd. manejar?
Yes, but I don't like to drive in heavy traffic.	Si, pero no me gusta manejar en tráfico pesado.
There are lots of cars on the street today.	Hay muchos carros en la calle hoy.

34

I am going to park the car near the door.	Voy a estacionar el carro cerca de la puerta.
You can help me pick out the groceries.	Vd. puede ayudarme escojer los abarrotes.
I am thirsty; let's have a soda.	Tengo sed; vamos a tomar una soda.
Bring a basket.	Traiga una canasta.
Get two cans of peas and two of corn.	Escoja dos latas de chícharos y dos de elote.
Large or small cans?	¿Latas grandes o chicas?
Medium, number three hundred.	Medianas, número tres cientos.
How many eggs do we have at home?	¿Cuantos blanquillos (huevos) tenemos en casa?
A dozen and a half.	Una docena y media.
That is enough.	Es bastante.
What else do we need?	¿Qué mas necesitamos?
A can of coffee and a loaf of bread.	Una lata de café y un pan pulman. (pieza de pan)
Do you want some gum?	¿Quiere Vd. chicle?
It is three thirty.	Son las tres y media.
Hurry up, we have to get home before four.	Ándale, tenemos que llegar a casa antes de las cuatro.
The children get home from school at four.	Los chamacos (niños) llegan a casa de la escuela a las cuatro.
They are afraid to be at home alone.	Tienen miedo de estar en casa solos.

35

I am going to stop the car on the side of the house.	Voy a parar (estacionar) el carro al lado de la casa.
Take the sacks inside.	Lleve los sacos adentro.
Wait, I will open the door.	Espere, Yo abro la puerta.
There come the kids.	Allá vienen los chamacos.
They are always hungry.	Siempre tienen hambre.
What do we have to give them?	¿Qué tenemos para darles?
I can make a roastbeef sandwich.	Puedo hacer un sanwich de rosbif.
Mama, I am hungry.	Mamá, tengo hambre.
Ask her if she wants some cookies and a glass of milk.	Pregúntele si quiere unas galletas y un vaso de leche.
The children do not want milk.	Los chamacos (hijos, niños) no quieren leche.
Give each one half of a Coca Cola.	Déle a cada uno media Coca Cola.
I have to pick up my husband.	Tengo que levantar mi esposo.
He gets off work at five thirty.	El sale del trabajo a las cinco y media.
You take care of Mary and John.	Vd. cuide a Maria y Juan.
Don't let them play in the street.	No los deje jugar en la calle.
They can play in the yard.	Pueden jujar en la yarda.

36

We want to eat at about six o'clock.	Queremos comer como a las seis.
The food is ready.	La comida está lista.
Put it on the table.	Póngala en la mesa.
This little girl is our neighbor's daughter.	Esta niña es hija de nuestro vecino.
She is going to eat with us.	Ella va a comer con nosotros.
Put a plate on for her.	Ponga un plato para ella.
Tomorrow is Sunday.	Mañana es domingo.
You don't have to do anything here.	Vd. no tiene que hacer nada aquí.
You can visit Gloria.	Puede visitar con Gloria.
I will take you over there.	Yo le llevo allá.
You and Gloria can go to the picture show if you like.	Vd. y Gloria pueden ir al cine si quieren.
The bus stops near the show.	El autobús para cerca del cine.
You ought to get home before night.	Deben llegar a casa antes de la noche.
It is dangerous to walk alone after dark.	Es peligrosa andar solos depues de obscurecerse.
Do you have any money?	¿Tiene Vd. dinero?
Yes, I have some.	Si, lo tengo.
Do you prefer to go to church?	¿Prefiere Vd. ir a la iglesia?

37

We can go to church in the morning and to the show in the afternoon.	Podemos ir a la iglesia por la mañana y al cine por la tarde.
There is a park down town.	Hay un parque en el centro.
You can take a walk around there if there is time.	Pueden dar una vuelta por allá si hay tiempo.
When you get back to Gloria's house, you can call me.	Al regresar a la casa de Gloria, puede llamarme.
Do you know this telephone number?	¿Sabe Vd. el número de este teléfono?
Write it on this paper and take it with you.	Escríbalo en este papel y llévelo consigo.

PUTTING UP THE GRO-CERIES	PONGA LOS ABARROTES
I will bring groceries to-day.	Traigo los abarrotes hoy.
Bring them from the car.	Tráigalos del carro.
Put all the sacks on the table.	Ponga todos los sacos en la mesa.
Put all the cans in the shelves.	Ponga todas las latas en los estantes.
Put the milk and butter in the refrigerator.	Ponga la mantequilla y leche en el enfriadero.
Wrap the meat in this paper.	Envuelve la carne en este papel.
Then put the meat in the deep freeze.	Entonces ponga ud la carne en el enfriadero para helar.
Put the fruit in the basket.	Ponga ud la fruta en el cesto.
There is a box in the refrigerator for the lettuce and carrots.	Hay un cajón en el enfriadero para la lechuga y las zanahorias.
Put the rice, beans and macaroni on this shelf.	Ponga el arroz, frijoles, y fideo en este estante.
Here is a basket for the potatoes and onions.	Aquí está una canasta para las papas y las cebollas.

CHAPTER XV

YARD WORK

John one day each week you will have to help Mrs. Wilson in the yard.	Juan, un día cada semana tiene que ayudar la señora Wilson en el jardín. (yarda)
Many Mexicans do not like to work in the yard but here it is necessary.	Muchos mexicanos no quieren trabajar en el jardín pero aquí es necesario.
First you have to cut the grass with this machine.	Primero tiene que cortar el sacate con esta máquina.
Then you must cut the grass with clippers that you cannot cut with the machine.	Entonces tiene que cortar el sacate con estas tijeras que no puede cortar con máquina.
In the flower beds there are weeds and grass you need to pull by hand.	En las camas (cuadras, bordes) de flores hay hierba y sacate que necesita sacar por la mano.
These flowers with wide leaves have to be trimmed with the clippers.	Estas flores con hojas anchas, tiene que cortar las puntas con las tijeras.
Today she wants new dirt on these flower beds.	Hoy ella quiere tierra nueva para estas camas de flores.
You may bring the dirt from the big canyon below the spring.	Vd. puede llevar la tierra del arroyo grande que esta abajo el ojo de agua.

40

When you pass the spring, gather me some water cress from the spring.	Cuando pase Vd. el ojo de agua, písqueme unos berros del ojo.
Carry a pick and shovel in the pick-up.	Lleve un pico y pala en la camioneta.
Bring dirt without grass and rocks.	Traiga Vd. tierra sin sacate y piedras.
By the side of the house she wants a ditch six inches deep and thirty feet long.	Por el lado de la casa quiere una zanja (ditche) de seis pulgadas de hondo y trienta pies de largo.
You may plant these flower seeds in the ditch and cover them with four inches of dirt.	Puede sembrar estas semillas de flores en la zanja y cubrirlas con cuatro pulgadas de tierra.
Let the ditch run full of water with the hose.	Deje salir la zanja llena de agua con la manguera.
In the garage there are shovels, hoes, hose, clippers, and other things you need to work in the yard.	En el garaje hay palas, azadas, mangueras, tijeras y otras cosas para trabajar en la yarda (el jardin).
You can use this rake to rake the leaves.	Puede usar este rastrillo para rastrear las hojas.
The carpet grass needs water.	El sacate carpeta necesita agua.
Put the sprinkler on the hose.	Ponga la regadera en la manguera.
The faucet is on the side of the house.	La llave está al lado de la casa.

The Bermuda grass is dry. Water it well.	El sacate chino está seco. Riéguelo bien.
Put the piles of grass and rakings into the wheel barrow.	Ponga los montones de sacate y recortes en l a carreta.
Take them to the garbage barrel behind the house.	Llévelos al barril de basura detrás de la casa.
The fertilizer is in the the garage.	El fertilizante (abono) está en el garaje.
Bring the sack and fill this bucket.	Traiga el saco y llene este bote.
Make holes for these shrubs four feet apart.	Haga pozos para estas matas cuatro pies de retirado.
Mix the fertilizer with the dirt.	Revuelva el abono con la tierra.
Work the soil well.	Trabaje bien la tierra.
Cover the roots well.	Cubra bien las raíces.
Be careful, these plants have thorns.	Tenga cuidado, estas plantas tienen espinas.
Cut the branches with this saw.	Corte las ramas con este serrucho.
Water with the hose running slowly near the plants.	Riegue con la manguera corriendo despacio cerquita a las plantas.
The ants are killing the flowers.	Las hormigas matan las flores.

Put poison in the ant hole (bed).	Ponga el veneno en el hormiguero.
Clean all the rocks out of the yard.	Quite todas las piedras del jardín.
Dig up the weeds by the roots.	Saque las hierbas de raíz.
This grass grows very fast.	Este sacate crece muy pronto.
The rose bushes grow better in the sun.	Los rosales crecen mejor en el sol.
Water them well.	Riéguelos bien.
Oil the lawn mower.	Ponga grasa en la máquina de cortar.
Clean well around the trees.	Limpie bien alrededor· de los árboles.
After forty minutes, change the sprinkler.	Después de cuarenta minutos, cambie la regadera.
The grass is tall here.	El zacate es alto aquí.
Make a flower bed in this corner.	Haga un borde para las flores en este rincón.

CHAPTER XVI

ILLNESS	ENFERMEDAD
I feel sick today.	Me siento malo hoy.
Do you have the flu?	¿Tiene Vd. la gripa?
I think I have a cold.	Pienso que tengo resfriado.
Take two aspirins now.	Tome dos mejorales ahora.
At noon, take two more.	Al media día, tome Vd. dos mas.
Stay in bed today.	Hoy guarde Vd. la cama.
Drink plenty of orange juice.	Tome Vd. bastante jugo de naranja.
Are you better now?	¿Siente Vd. un mejor ahora?
I feel about the same.	Me siento lo mismo.
I think you have the flu.	Creo que Vd. tiene la gripa.
Take two of these pills.	Tome Vd. estas dos pildoras.
Tonight you take two more.	Esta noche tome Vd. dos mas.
How are you today?	¿Como está Vd. hoy?
I feel much better.	Me siento mucho mejor.
You may stay in your room today.	Vd puede guardar su cuarto hoy.
If you leave the room, wear a coat.	Si sale de su cuarto lleve un saco.
I think you may work tomorrow.	Pienso que Vd. pueda trabajar mañana.

This is for your upset stomach.	Este es para su estómago envuelto.
Shake bottle and take two tablespoons.	Agite la botella y tome dos cucharas.
Do you feel better now?	¿Siente Vd. mejor?
These pills are for your cold.	Estas pildoras son para su resfriado.
Take two every four hours during the day.	Tome dos cada cuatro horas durante el día.
I will take you to the doctor.	Le llevo Vd. al doctor.
Go to your house and dress.	Vaya Vd. a su casa para vestirse.
I feel ill.	Me siento malo.
Did you rest well?	¿Durmió bien?
You have a cut on your finger.	Tiene cortado en el dedo.
Bring me the Iodine.	Tráigame Vd. el yodo.
Paint the wound with this stick.	Pinte Vd. la herida con este palito.
Now put this band aid around the finger.	Ponga este band-aid alrededor el dedo.
Leave it on until tomorrow.	Déjelo hasta mañana.
Do you have a headache?	¿Tiene Vd. dolor de cabeza?
Yes, I do have a headache.	Sí, tengo dolor de cabeza.

45

Take two anacin pills.	Tome Vd. dos pildoras de anacin.
Take a nap for two hours.	Tome Vd. una siesta de dos horas.
You have something in your eye.	Vd tiene algo en su ojo.
We will put some drops of murine in the eye.	Ponemos unas gotas de murine en el ojo.
Put your head back.	Ponga la cabeza atrás..
Move your eye from side to side.	Mueva vd el ojo de un lado al otro.
It is a piece of straw.	Es Vd. pedazo de paja.
I can get it out with this paper napkin.	Yo puedo sacarlo con esta servilleta de papel.
I have the stomach ache.	Tengo dolor del estómago.
Put this alka-seltzer in a glass of water.	Ponga esta alka-seltezer en un vaso de agua.
Drink it when it quits foaming.	Tómelo cuando no hay espuma.
You will feel better soon.	Vd siente mejor pronto.

CHAPTER XVII

THE FURNITURE	LOS MUEBLES
ash tray	cenicero
armchair	sillón
bed	cama
bedspread	sobrecamas
blankets	frazadas
bookcase	estante
bookrack	librero
broom	escoba
candlestick	candelero
chair	silla
chair, rocking	silla mecedora
chandelier	arana de luces
clock	reloj
clothes dryer	secadora de ropa
coffee table	cafeto
cookie jar	jarra de cocina
cushion	cojín
deep freeze	enfriadero
dining table	comedor
dish-washer	lava platos
dresser	tocador
flower pot	maceta
gun cabinet	vitrina de armas
iron	plancha
ironing board	tabla de planchar
lamp	lámpara
light	luz
mattress	colchón
mirror	espejo
mop	trapo
napkins, large	servilletas
napkin, small	toallita
night stand	burol
outdoor furniture	muebles de patio
piano	piano
pictures	cuadros

47

pillow	almohada
pillow case	funda de almohada
place mat	tapete
radio	radio
refrigerator	enfriedera
rug	alfombra
sheets	sábanas
sewing machine	máquina de coser
sofa	sofá
stove	estufa
table	mesa
television	televición
towel	toalla
typewriter	máquina de escribir
vaccum cleaner	aspirador de polvo
vase	vaso
washing machine	lavadora
writing desk	escritorio

GROCERY LIST	LOS COMESTIBLES
apple	manzana
apricot	albaricoque
asparagus	espárrago
barbeque	barbacoa
bacon	tocino
baking powder	resol
banana	plátano banana
beans	frijoles
beans (string)	ejote
beef steak	bif stek
beer	cerveza
beets	betabeles
bread	pan
brocoli	bróculi
brussel sprouts	repollo chiquito
butter	mantequilla
cabbage	repollo
cake	pastel
candy	dulce
canteloupe	melón
carrots	zanahorias
cauliflower	coliflor
celery	apio
cheese	queso
cherry	cereza
chicken	gallina
coconut	coco
chili	chili
coffee	café
corn	helote
cracker	galleta
crumb	miga
cucumber	pepino

desert	postre
duck	pato
egg	huevo blanquillo
eggplant	verenja
enchilladas	enchilladas
figs	higos
fish	pescados
flour	harina
fruit	fruta
fryer	pollo
garlic	ajo
grape	uva
grapefruit	toronja
ham	jamón
hen	gallina
hog	puerco marrano
honey	miel
ice	hielo
ice cream	helado nieve
juice	jugo
kid goat	cabrito
lamb	cordero
lamb chops	chuletas de cordero
lard	manteca
lemon	limón
lettuce	lechuga
lime	lima
liver	hígado
macaroni	macarrones fideo
mangos	mangos
meat	carne
milk	leche
molasses	melaza
mustard	mostaza
nut	nuez
oatmeal	avena
okra	bombones
onion	cebolla
orange	naranja

parsley	perejil
pea	chícharo
peach	durazno melocotón
peanut	cacahuate
pear	pera
pecans	nueces
pepper (black)	pimiento
pepper (green)	chili verde
pepper (bell)	chili dulce
pineapple	piña
plums	ciruelas
popcorn	palomitas
pork chops	chuletas de puerco
potato	papa
pot roast	carne de horno
preserves	conservas
quail	codorniz
radish	rábano
rice	arroz
roast beef	bif asada
roasting ears	helotes
salt	sal
sardines	sardina
salmon	salmón
shrimp	camarones
soup	caldo
spaghetti	fideo
spinach	acelga espinaca
squash	calabaza
strawberry	fresa
sugar	azúcar
tacos	tacos
tomato	tomate
toast	pan tostada
turkey	guajolote cocono
turnip	nabo
vegetables	legumbres
vinegar	vinagre
yams	camote

51

CHAPTER XIX

THE CLOTHES	LA ROPA
belt	cinto
brassiere	brasier
blouse	blusa
bonnet	capota
boot	botas
cap	gorro
clothes	ropa
coat	saco
collar	cuello
drawers	calzones
dress	vestido
garter belt	liga liguero
girdle	faja
gloves	guantes
half slip	media fondo
hat	sombrero
house shoes	sandalias pantuflas
jacket	chaqueta
night gown	camizón
overcoat	abrigo sobretodo
pajamas	pijamas
pants	pantalones
pantie hose	pantie media
purse	bolsa
robe	bata
scarf	chalina
shirt	camisa
shoes	zapatos
shorts	pantalones cortas
slip	fondo
socks	calcetines
stockings	medias
suit	traje
skirt	falda
sweater	sweter chamara
tie	corbata
underclothes	ropa interior
undershirt	camiseta

THE COLORS **CHAPTER XX**

blonde	rubia
blue	azul
brown	café
golden	dorado
black	negro
gray	gris
green	verde
orange	anaranjado
pink	rosa
purple	morado
rose	rosa (color de rosa)
red	roja
silver color	plateado
violet	violeta
white	blanco
yellow	amarillo

HUMAN ANATOMY

ankle	tobillo	fingernail	uña
artery	artería	forehead	frente
arm	brazo	hair	cabello
back	espalda	hand	mano
backbone	espina dorsal	head	cabeza
blood	sangre	heart	corazón
body	cuerpo	heel	talón
brains	sesos	hip	cadera
cheek	mejilla	jaw	quijada
chin	barba	knee	rodilla
ear	oreja	leg	pierna
inner ear	oído	lips	labios
elbow	codo	lungs	pulmones
eyes	ojos	mouth	boca
eyebrow	ceja	neck	cuello
eyelash	pestaña	nerves	nervios
eyelid	párpado	nose	nariz
face	cara	skin	piel
feet	pies	sore	grano
finger	dedo	stomach	estómago
		toes	dedos

CHAPTER XXI
GREETINGS AND COURTESIES

Congratulations.	Felicidades.
Happy Birthday.	Feliz cumpleaños.
Happy Anniversary.	Feliz aniversario.
Merry Christmas.	Feliz Navidad.
New Year's Greetings.	Feliz Año Nuevo.
Easter Greetings.	Felices Pascuas.
Thank you.	Muchas gracias.
Pardon, please.	Perdone, por favor.
You are welcome.	Por (De) nada.
Pardon me.	Perdone me.
Good morning.	Buenas días.
Good afternoon.	Buenas tardes.
Good night.	Buenas noches.
It is cold (warm) today.	Hace frío (calor) hoy.
How are you feeling?	¿Cómo le va?
I feel ill.	Me siento malo.
I feel fine.	Me siento bien.
Did you rest well?	¿Durmió bien?
My sympathy to you.	Le acompaño en su pesar.
I am very sorry.	Cuánto lo siento.
I will return.	Ya vuelvo.
Come in, please.	Pase Vd. , por favor.

CHAPTER XXII
GENERAL CONVERSATION

What do you want?	¿Que desea Vd.?
You are very kind.	Vd. es muy amable.
That pleases me.	Eso me gusta.
Don't forget.	No se olvide.
All right.	Está bueno.
I don't understand.	No entiendo.
Come here, please.	Por favor, venga acá.
It is getting late.	Se hace tarde.
Let's go home.	Vámonos a casa.
Do you have a paper sack?	¿Tiene una bolsa de papel?
Can you tell me what time it is?	¿Me puede decir que hora es?
A match, please.	Un fósforo, por favor.
This will be all.	Esto será todo.
How much do you need?	¿Cuánto necesitas?
Please wrap it up.	Envuélvalo por favor.
What do you mean?	¿Que quiere decir?
This will do.	Este está bueno.
What is the matter with you?	¿Qué tiene Vd.?

56

A great deal.	Mucho.
Every other day.	Cada otro día.
Hurry up.	Tenga prisa.
Once more.	Una mas.
I do not care.	No le hace conmigo.
Let us take a walk.	Vamos a pasearnos.
Let us take a ride.	Vamos a pasearnos en carro.
Look out.	Cuídele Vd.
From time to time.	De vez en cuando.
Bring them now.	Tráigalos ahora.
Are you happy here?	¿Está Vd. alegre aqui?
Come to work at 8:00 in the morning.	Venga a trabajar a las ocho de la mañana.

CHAPTER XXIII

SUBJECT PRONOUNS

Yo	I	Nosotros, Nosotras	We
Usted	You	Ustedes	You (Plural)
Él	He	Ellos	They (Masculine)
Ella	She	Ellas	They (Feminine)

"Nosotros" refers to male persons, or a mixed group.

"Nosotras" refers to female persons.

"Ellos" refers to male things or a mixed group.

"Ellas" refers to female things.

"Tu" and "vosotros" (pl) are subject pronouns that mean "you". They are correctly used only when speaking to members of the family, intimate acquaintances, and servants. There is also a form of the verb which is used under the same conditions. They are being omitted from this book.

CARDINAL NUMBERS

cero	0	cincuenta	50
uno, a	1	cincuenta y uno	51
dos	2	cincuenta y dos	52
tres	3	sesenta	60
cuatro	4	sesenta y uno	61
cinco	5	sesenta y dos	62
seis	6	setenta	70
siete	7	setenta y uno	71
ocho	8	setenta y dos	72
nueve	9	ochenta	80
diez	10	ochenta y uno	81
once	11	ochenta y dos	82
doce	12	noventa	90
trece	13	noventa y uno	91
catorce	14	noventa y dos	92
quince	15	ciento (cien)	100
diez y seis	16	ciento uno	101
diez y siete	17	ciento dos	102
diez y ocho	18	doscientos, as	200
diez y nueve	19	trescientos, as	300
veinte	20	cuatrocientos, as	400
veinte y uno	21	quinientos, as	500
veinte y dos	22	seiscientos, as	600
veinte y tres	23	setecientos, as	700
treinta	30	ochocientos, as	800
treinta y uno	31	novecientos, as	900
treinta y dos	32	mil	1,000
cuarenta	40	dos mil	2,000
cuarenta y uno	41	tres mil	3,000
cuarenta y dos	42	un millón	1,000,000

59

ORDINAL NUMBERS

primero	first
segundo	second
tercero	third
cuarto	fourth
quinto	fifth
sexto	sixth
séptimo	seventh
octavo	eighth
noveno	ninth
décimo	tenth

TIME EXPRESSIONS

Months of Year

enero	January
febrero	February
marzo	March
abril	April
mayo	May
junio	June
julio	July
agosto	August
septiembre	September
octubre	October
noviembre	November
diciembre	December

Days of Week

lunes	Monday
martes	Tuesday
miércoles	Wednesday
jueves	Thursday
viernes	Friday
sábado	Saturday
domingo	Sunday

Seasons of Year

la primavera	spring
el verano	summer
el otoño	autumn
el invierno	winter

TIME EXPRESSIONS

second	segundo
minute	minuto
half-hour	media hora
hour	hora
morning	mañana
noon	mediodía
afternoon	tarde
evening	tarde
night	noche
midnight	medianoche
today	hoy
What time is it?	¿Qué hora es?
It is four o'clock.	Son las cuatro.
What time is it?	¿Qué hora son?
It is one o'clock.	Es la una.
last week.	la semana pasada.
next week.	la semana que viene (entra).
yesterday afternoon.	ayer por la tarde.

yesterday morning .	ayer por la mañana.
tomorrow afternoon.	mañana por la tarde.
tomorrow morning.	mañana por la mañana.
it is late.	es tarde.
it is early.	es temprano.
day after tomorrow.	pasado mañana.
day before yesterday.	ante ayer
a little later.	un poco despues.
two thirty.	dos y media.
at the end of the month.	al fin del mes.
from time to time.	de vez en cuando.
at about two o'clock.	como a las dos.
a little while ago.	hace poco.
two years ago.	hace dos años.

at sunset.	a la caída del sol.
At what time?	¿A qué hora?
What day of the month is today?	¿Que día del mes es hoy?
It is three thirty.	Son las tres y media.
It is 8:15 o'clock.	Son las ocho y quince.
It is 10 A. M.	Son las diez de la mañana.
At one o'clock in the afternoon.	A la una de la tarde.
At two o'clock in the morning.	A las dos de la mañana.

In a question in Spanish, the subject generally follows the verb:

Where is the bucket?	¿Donde está el bote?
The bucket is here.	El bote está aquí.
Why didn't you come yesterday?	¿Por qué no vino Vd. ayer?
I did not finish picking.	No terminé la pisca.
Does the tractor run good?	¿Anda bien el tractor?
Yes, it is very good.	Si, es muy bueno.

PRESENT TENSE

The infinitive of all verbs in Spanish ends in "ar", "er", or "ir". The present tense expresses action at the present time. It is formed by adding the following endings to the stem of the verb. The stem of the verb is found by cutting off the "ar", "er", or "ir".

AR verbs	ER verbs	IR verbs
o - amos	o - emos	o - imos
a - an	e - en	e - en

Hablar - To Speak

yo hablo

Vd.   )
él   )   habla
ella   )

nosotros)   hablamos
nosotras)

Vds.   )
ellos   )   hablan
ellas   )

Vender - To Sell

vendo	vendemos
vende	venden

Vivir - To Live

vivo	vivimos
vive	viven

"Yo hablo" may be translated "I speak", "I do speak", or "I am speaking".

"Vd. habla" may be translated "You speak", "You do speak", or "You are speaking".

65

POSSESSIVE ADJECTIVES

mi, mis - my		nuestro, a	)	our
		nuestros, as	)	
su, sus - your		su, sus	-	your
su, sus - his		su, sus	-	their
su, sus - her		su, sus	-	their

Like other adjectives, the possessive adjectives
agree with the noun in gender and number.

mi casa	my house
mi hijo	my son
mis casas	my houses
mis hijos	my sons
su casa	your house
su casa	his house
su casa	her house
sus casas	your houses
sus casas	his houses
sus casas	her houses
su hijo	your son
su hijo	his son
su hijo	her son
sus hijos	your sons
sus hijos	his sons
sus hijos	her sons
nuestra casa	our house
nuestras casas	our houses
nuestro hijo	our son
nuestros hijos	our sons
su casa	their house
sus casas	their houses
su hijo	their son
sus hijos	their sons

Since the word "su" has several meanings, the meaning may be made clear by using "de" with the proper pronoun as follows:

su casa de él	his house
la casa de él	his house
su casa de ella	her house
la casa de ella	her house
sus casas de él	his houses
las casas de él	his houses
sus casas de ella	her houses
las casas de ella	her houses
su casa de Vd.	your house
la casa de Vd.	your house
su casa de ellos	their house
la casa de ellas	their house
sus casas de Vd.	your houses
las casas de Vd.	your houses
sus casas de ellos	their houses
las casas de ellas	their houses

You will notice from the examples above that when the prepositional pronoun is used after the noun, the definite article (the) may be used before the noun instead of the possessive adjective.

DIRECT OBJECT PRONOUNS

A direct object receives the action of the verb directly. This means it is acted upon by the subject.

| I hit <u>John</u>. | I hit <u>him</u>. |

me	-	me	nos	-	us
le	-	you (mas.)	los	-	you (pl.)
la	-	you (fem.)	las	-	you (pl.)
le	-	him	los	-	them (mas.)
la	-	her, it (fem.)	las	-	them (fem,)
lo	-	him, it (mas.)			

The direct object pronoun comes immediately before the verb.

Él compró las vacas.	He bought the cows.
Él las compró.	He bought them.
Yo la veo.	I see her.
Yo veo el hombre.	I see the man.
Yo le (lo) veo.	I see him.
Yo veo las vacas.	I see the cows.
Yo las veo.	I see them.
Vendí los chivos.	I sold the goats.
Los vendí.	I sold them.

After an infinitive, affirmative command, and a present participle, the object pronoun is generally placed after the verb and attached to it.

Quiero vender las vacas.	I want to sell the cows.
Quiero venderlas.	I want to sell them.
Traiga los sacos.	Bring the sacks.
Tráigalos.	Bring them.
Él está cortando las yerbas.	He is cutting the weeds.
Él está cortándolas.	He is cutting them.

PREPOSITIONAL PRONOUNS

Prepositional pronouns are those that are used after a preposition.

mí	-	me	nosotros, as	-	us
Vd.	-	you	Vds.	-	you
él	-	him	ellos	-	them
ella	-	her	ellas	-	them

They are the same as the subject pronouns except "mi" is used instead of "yo".

El dinero es para Vd.	The money is for you.
El dinero es para él.	The money is for him.

69

PAST (PRETERITE) TENSE

The past tense expresses past time. This means something that has already happened. The principal past tense (preterite) is formed by adding the following endings to the stem of the verb.

AR verbs	ER verbs	IR verbs
é - amos	í - imos	í - imos
ó - aron	ió - ieron	ió - ieron

Hablar - To Speak

yo hablé	hosotros, as hablamos
Vd. habló	Vds. hablaron
el habló	ellos hablaron
ella habló	ellas hablaron

Vender - To Sell

vendi	vendimos
vendio	vendieron

Vivir - To Live

vivi	vivimos
vivio	vivieron

Yo hablé ayer.	I spoke yesterday.
El habló ayer.	He spoke yesterday.
Juan vendió la vaca.	John sold the cow.

There are other past tenses, but the preterite is used most. You can get along very well without the other tenses.

FUTURE TENSE

There is a future tense. However, future time can be expressed by using the present tense of the verb "ir" (to go) before the infinitive of the verb. The infinitive is preceded by "a"

Voy a topear betabeles mañana.	I am going to top beets tomorrow.
El va a cultivar el algodón.	He is going to plow the cotton.

The present tense may also be used to express action not yet completed.

Rodeamos mañana.	We round up tomorrow.
Yo le hablo mas tarde.	I will talk to you later.

OTHER EXPLANATIONS

The auxiliary (helping) words "do" and "does" do not exist in Spanish, but are translated as a part of the main verb itself.

¿Tiene Vd. dinero?	Do you have any money?
No, no tengo dinero.	No, I do not have any money.
¿Vive él aquí?	Does he live here?

You can ask the name of things with this question:

¿Cómo se llama esto?	What is the name of this?
¿Cómo se llama Vd.?	What is your name?

71

You may also find out the meaning of a word by using the question: ¿Cómo se dice?

¿Cómo se dice "go" en español?	How do you say "go" in Spanish?
¿Cómo se dice "this" en español?	How do you say "this" in Spanish?

DEMONSTRATIVE ADJECTIVES

este	this	estos	these
esta	this	estas	these

ese	that	esos	those
esa	that	esas	those

Este arado es nuevo.	This plow is new.
Esta plancha está caliente.	This iron is hot.
Estos arados son nuevos.	These plows are new.
Estas planchas están calientes.	These irons are hot.
Ese caballo is mio.	That horse is mine.
Esa vaca es gorda.	That cow is fat.
Esas vacas son gordas.	Those cows are fat.

aquel	that	aquellos	those
aquella	that	aquellas	those

These words for "that" and "those" are not used as much as "ese". They refer to something far away.

Aquel hombre en Nueva York.	That man in New York.

Demonstrative adjectives agree with the noun they modify in gender and number.

73

COMMAND FORM OF VERBS

To tell a person to do or not to do a thing (give a command), you use the command form of the verb. It is formed by adding these endings to the stem of the verb. There are only two endings, a singular and a plural, because you are always talking to one person (singular) or more than one (plural).

Ar verbs	ER verbs	IR verbs
e - en	a - an	a - an
hablar	comer	escribir
hable	coma	escriba
hablen	coman	escriban

Hable Vd. más despacio.	Speak slower.
Hablen Vds. más des-pacio.	Speak slower.
Corte el sacate.	Cut the grass.
Venda Vd. la vaca.	Sell the cow.
Vendan Vds. la vaca.	Sell the cow.
Coma Vd. la carne.	Eat the meat.
Coman Vds. la carne.	Eat the meat.
Escriba Vd. su nombre.	Write your name.
Escriban Vds. su nombre.	Write your name.

INDIRECT OBJECT PRONOUNS

An indirect object is the person to whom or for whom the action of the verb is completed.

me - to me	nos - to us
le - to you	les - to you (pl)
le - to him	les - to them
le - to her	

Yo dí la carta a Juan.	I gave the letter to John.
Yo le dí la carta.	I gave the letter to him.
Juan manda dinero a Maria.	John sends money to Mary.
Juan le manda dinero.	John sends money to her.

Since "le" and "les" have more than one meaning, the meaning may be made clear by using "a" with the prepositional pronoun after the verb.

Yo le dí el libro a él (ella, Vd.).	I gave the book to him, (her, you).

The indirect object pronoun precedes the direct object pronoun when both are used in the same sentence.

Él me lo dió.	He gave it to me.
Ellos me los dieron.	They gave them to me.

GRAMMAR SECTION
Gender of Nouns

A noun is the name of a person, place or thing.
In Spanish all nouns are masculine or feminine. Nouns
ending in "o" are masculine, and those ending in "a" are
feminine. The names of female beings are feminine.
There is no rule for determining the gender of other
nouns. The plural of nouns is formed by adding "s" to
those ending in a vowel (a, e, i, o, u) and "es" to
all others.

The Definite Articles

There are four words that mean "the" :

el   the (used with masculine singular nouns)
       el libro - the book; el hombre - the man

la   the (used with feminine singular nouns)
       la casa - the house; la mujer - the woman

los   the (used with masculine plural nouns)
       los libros - the books; los hombres - the men

las   the (used with feminine plural nouns)
       las casas - the houses; las mujeres - the
       women

Gender and Number of Adjectives

An adjective is a word that describes or limits
a noun. An adjective agrees with the noun it modifies
in gender and number. Adjectives, like nouns, are
all masculine or feminine. Those ending in "o" form
the feminine by changing the "o" to "a". Adjectives
that do not end in "o" or "a" have only a singular and
plural. The plural of an adjective if formed by adding
"s" to those ending in a vowel and "es" to those ending
in a consonant. When you wish to describe anything,
put the adjective after the noun - the reverse of
English. Other adjectives precede the noun.

el toro negro	the black bull
los toros negros	the black bulls
la vaca negra	the black cow
las vacas negras	the black cows
el libro verde	the green book
los libros verdes	the green books
la pluma verde	the green pea
las plumas verdes	the green peas
el libro azul	the blue book
los libros azules	the blue books
la vaca azul	the blue cow
las vacas azules	the blue cows
mucho dinero	much money
mucha comida	much food
muchas vacas	many cows
muchos chivos	many goats

Possession of Nouns

The possession of nouns corresponding to the English 's or s' (apostrophe s, or s apostrophe) is espressed in Spanish by use of the preposition "de" placed before the possessor. There is no such thing in Spanish as Juan's libro (John's book), but el libro de Juan (the book of John).

Idiomatic Expressions

The verb "tener" is used to mean "to be" in some instances, such as:

Tengo frío.	I am cold.
Él tiene calor.	He is hot.
Tengo sed.	I am thirsty.
Ella tiene hambre.	She is hungry.
¿Tiene sueño?	Are you sleepy?
El tiene prisa.	He is in a hurry.

77

Hacer (to do or make) is used to express
weather conditions and periods of time.

Hace frío.	It is cold.
Hace calor.	It is hot.
Hace dos días.	Two days ago.
Hace una semana.	A week ago.

Other Expressions

Por favor.	Please.
En seguida.	Immediately.
Con permiso.	Excuse me.
Ir de compras.	To go shopping.
Me gusta la carne.	I like the meat.
¿Le gustan las peras?	Do you like pears?

Uses of the Verbs "ser" and "estar"

There are two verbs that mean "to be" in
Spanish: "Estar" is used to show location or po-
sition, the place where a person or thing is and
to express a temporary condition. "Ser" is used
at all other times, such as to show age, ownership,
occupation, time expressions, nationality, a natural
or inherent condition, etc.

El caballo está en el corral.
The horse is in the pen.

El es vaquero.
He is a cowboy.

La carne está caliente.
The meat is hot.

Este caballo es mío.
This horse is mine.

La vaca es vieja.
The cow is old.

¿Qué hora es?
What time is it?

Juan es mejicano.
John is a Mexican.

Sus ojos son verdes.
His eyes are green.

78

Present Participle

The present participle is the form of the verb that ends in "ing" in English. The present participle is formed in Spanish by adding "ando" to the stem of "ar" verbs and "iendo" to the stem of "er" and "ir" verbs.

hablar - to speak	comer - to eat
hablando - speaking	comiendo - eating

vivir - to live
viviendo - living

Estar may be used with the present participle to express progressive action.

Él está regando.	He is irrigating.
Las vacas están comiendo.	The cows are eating.

Accentuation

In pronouncing words of more than one syllable, you raise your voice higher on one part or syllable of the word. This is called the accented syllable. Long words are easier to pronounce if you say the word one part (syllable) at a time. Words ending in a vowel (a, e, i, o, u) or "n" or "s" are accented on next to the last syllable. All other words are accented on the last part (syllable). The exception to this rule will have a written accent mark (') on the syllable to be accented.

In dividing a word into parts (syllables), a consonant is generally followed by a vowel; consonants are separated. The following words are divided into syllables, and the accented syllable is underlined.

me-sa	sa-lud	ca-fé	to-ma-te	a-cá
do-lar	tra-ba-jo	pa-sa-por-te	má-qui-na	

"It" as a Subject

When used as a subject in a sentence, "it" is not expressed, but is understood.

Es temprano.	It is early.
Es tarde.	It is late.
Es necesario.	It is necessary.

"Despues de" and "Antes de"

"Despues de" (after) and "antes de" (before) are followed by an infinitive.

Antes de acostarse, apague Vd. la luz.
Before going to bed, put out the light.

Después de comer, venga a la casa.
After eating, come to the house.

IRREGULAR VERBS

Many of the commonly used verbs are irregular. That means that they are not spelled in the regular way. A few of the most useful irregular verbs follow.

Tener - To Have

Present Tense

yo tengo	nosotros, as tenemos
Vd. tiene	Vds. tienen
él tiene	ellos tienen
ella tiene	ellas tienen

Past Tense

tuve	tuvimos
tuvo	tuvieron
tuvo	tuvieron
tuvo	tuvieron

Command

tenga Vd.	tengan Vds.

Decir - To Say, Tell

Present Tense

digo	decimos
dice	dicen

Past Tense

dije	dijimos
dijo	dijeron

Command

diga	digan

Ser - To Be

Present Tense

soy	somos
es	son

Past Tense

fuí	fuimos
fué	fueron

Command

sea	sean

Ir - To Go

Present Tense

voy	vamos
va	van

Past Tense

fuí	fuimos
fué	fueron

Command

vaya	vayan

Estar - To Be

Present Tense

estoy	estamos
está	están

Past Tense

estuve	estuvimos
estuvo	estuvieron

Command

esté	estén

Venir - To Come

Present Tense

vengo	venimos
viene	vienen

Past Tense

vine	vinimos
vino	vinieron

Command

venga	vengan

Traer - To Bring

Present Tense

traigo	traemos ·
trae	traen

Past Tense

traje	trajimos
trajo	trajeron

Command

traiga	traigan

Poner - To Put

Present Tense

pongo	ponemos
pone	ponen

Past Tense

puse	pusimos
puso	pusieron

Command

ponga	pongan

Hacer - To Do, To Make

Present Tense

hago	hacemos
hace	hacen

Past Tense

hice	hicimos
hizo	hicieron

Command

haga	hagan

Querer - To Want, To Wish

Present Tense

quiero	queremos
quiere	quieren

Past Tense

quise	quisimos
quiso	quisieron

Command

quiera	quieran

Dar - To Give

Present Tense

doy	damos
da	dan

Past Tense

dí	dimos
dió	dieron

Command

dé	den

Ver - To See

Present Tense

veo	vemos
ve	ven

Past Tense

ví	vimos
vió	vieron

Command

vea	vean

CHAPTER XXIV

SPANISH -- ENGLISH VOCABULARY

A

a -- to, at
abajo -- under, below, down
abandonado -- abandoned
abanico, -- fan
abeja, f -- bee
abierto -- open
abril, m -- April
abrir -- to open
abuela, f -- grandmother
abuelo, m -- grandfather
acá -- here
acabar -- to end, finish
acequia, f -- ditch
acelga, f -- spinach
aceite, m -- oil
acercarse -- to approach, come near
acompañar -- to accompany
acre, m -- acre
adelante -- forward, ahead
aflojar -- to relax, loosen
agosto, m, -- August
agua, f (el) -- water
aguja, f -- needle
ahí -- there (by you)

ahora -- now
ahorita -- right now
ajo, m -- garlic
al -- to the, at the
alambre, m -- wire
alambre de pico -- barb wire
albaricoque -- apricot
alfanje, m -- scythe
al fin -- at last, finally
alemán, m -- German man
alfombra, f -- rug
algo -- something
algodón -- cotton
alguien -- somebody
alguna -- some
alguna vez -- ever, sometime
alimento, m -- food
almacén, m -- wholesale house
almárcigo, m -- seed bed
almohada, f -- pillow
alto -- tall, high, halt
alumno (a) -- pupil, student

allá -- there, over
   yonder
allí -- there
amanecer, m --
   dawn (to dawn)
amarillo -- yellow
americano (a) --
   American
amigo (a) -- friend
andar -- to walk
anillo, m -- ring
animales, m -- animals
Anita -- Annie
año, m -- year
año nuevo, m --
   New Year
anoche -- last night
anochecer -- to
   grow dark
anteanoche -- night
   before last
anteayer -- day before
   yesterday
anterior -- former,
   preceding
antes -- before (adj.)
antes de -- before
   (preposition)
apartamiento -- apart-
   ment
apio, m -- celery
aprender -- to learn
aquí -- here
arado, m -- plow
archivar -- to file
archivo, m -- file,
   archive

arena, f -- sand
arrestar -- to arrest
arroz, m -- rice
asiento, m -- seat
asiento de atras --
   back seat
asiento de enfrente --
   front seat
aspirador de polvo --
   vacuum
atrás -- behind, back,
   past
aún -- ever, still,
   yet, as yet
aunque -- although
auto, m -- auto, car
automóvil, m -- auto-
   mobile
ave, f -- fowl
avena, f -- oat
avenida, f -- avenue
ayer -- yesterday
ayudar -- to help
azada, f; azadón, f--
   hoe
azúcar, m -- sugar
azul -- blue

B

baile, m -- dance
bajar -- to lower,
   get down
bajo -- low, short,
   underneath
bala -- bale
baño, m -- bath
barbacoa -- barbecue

88

barra, f -- crowbar
bástago, m -- top (plants)
bastante -- enough
bastar -- to be enough
basura -- trash
bata -- robe
beber -- to drink
becerro, m -- calf
betabeles, m -- beets
bien -- well
bif asada -- roast
  beef
bif stek -- beef steak
blanco -- white
blanquillo, m --
  egg
blusa, f -- blouse
bodega, f -- packing
  shed, warehouse
bonito -- pretty
boquilla, f -- gap
bordear -- to bed
  plants
bordo, m -- border,
  bed, edge
borrega, f -- ewe
  sheep
bote, m -- boat,
  bucket
botella, f -- bottle
bracero -- contract
  laborer
brincar -- to jump
bróculi, m -- broccoli
bujía -- spark plug
bunche, m -- bunch
burro -- donkey

C

caber -- fit into, to
  contain
cabra, f -- goat
cabeza, f -- head
cabrito, m -- kid
  (goat)
cacahuate -- peanut
cada -- each, every
caer -- to fall
cafeto -- coffee table
café -- brown, coffee,
  café
cafetera -- coffee pot
caja -- box
calabaza -- squash
calentador, -- heater
caliente -- warm
calle, f -- street
calzones -- under-
  wear, panties
cama, f -- bed
camarones -- shrimp
caminar -- to travel
camino, m -- road
camiseta -- under-
  shirt
camisa, f -- shirt
camizón -- nightgown
camote, m -- sweet
  potato
campo, m -- country,
  field
canasta, f -- basket
canasto, m -- large
  basket
canoa, f -- canoe,
  trough

cansado -- tired
cantina, f -- saloon
capote -- cape
carburador, m -- carburator
cárcel, f -- jail
careces, m -- fly blows
carga, f -- load, cargo, freight
cargador, m -- loader
Carlos -- Charles
carne -- meat
carretera, f -- highway
carretilla -- wheel barrow
carro, m -- car, auto
carta, f -- letter
casa, f -- house
cascabel, m -- bell, rattlesnake
cascajo, m -- gravel
cazar -- to hunt
cazuela, f -- pan
cebolla, f -- onion
cedro, f -- cedar
cementera, f -- hay stack
cemento, m -- cement
cenicero -- ash tray
cepillo -- brush
cerca, f -- fence
cerca (adv.) -- near
cerca de (prep.) -- near
cereza -- cherry

cerrado -- closed
cerrillo, f -- match
certificado, m -- certificate
cerveza, f -- beer
chalina -- scarf
chaqueta, f -- jacket
chícharo -- pea
chicle -- chewing gum
chile, m -- pepper
chile verde, m -- green pepper
chile dulce -- bell pepper
chile -- chile
chivo, m -- goat
chocar -- to collide
chofer -- driver, chauffeur
choque, m -- wreck
chorizo, m -- sausage
chuleta, f -- chop (meat)
chuletas de cordero -- lamb chops
chuletas de puerco -- pork chops
cicatriz, f -- scar
cierto -- certain
cigarro -- cigarette
cine, m -- picture show
cireulas -- plums
cita, f -- date, engagement

ciudad, f -- city
ciudadanía, f --
citizenship
ciudadano (a) --
citizen
claramente -- clearly
claro -- clear
cobija, f -- blanket
cobrar -- to collect,
charge
coche -- car, coach
cocino -- kitchen
coco -- coconut
cócono, m -- turkey
codorniz, f -- quail
coliflor -- cauliflower
colocar -- place
color, m -- color
comedor -- dining
room
comer -- to eat
comerciante, m --
merchant
comida, f -- dinner,
food
como -- as, like
¿cómo? -- how?
cómodo -- comfortable
compañero (a) --
companion
compañía, f -- company
comprar -- to buy
con -- with
condado, m -- county
conducir -- to conduct
lead

conejo, m -- rabbit
conmigo -- with me
conocer -- to be
acquainted with
conocido (a) --
acquaintance
copas -- dessert
dishes
conseguir -- to
get, obtain
cónsul, m -- consul
consulado, m --
consulate
conservas -- preserves
construir -- to
construct
contento -- contented
contestar -- to
answer
contigo -- with you
(fam)
corbata, f -- necktie
cordero, m -- lamb
cordón, f -- cord,
string
codorniz -- quail
corral, m -- pen
correo, m -- post
office, mail
cortar -- to cut,
to mow
cortinas, f -- curtains
corto -- short
cosa, f -- thing
cosecha, f -- harvest

91

cosechar -- to harvest
costal, m -- sack
corbata -- tie
coyote, m -- coyote
crecer -- to grow
creer -- to believe,
    think
crema, f -- cream
criar -- to raise
cruz, f -- cross
cruzar -- to cross
¿cuál? -- which?
¿cuándo? -- when?
cuánto? -- how much?
¿cuántos? -- how many?
cuarto, m -- room,
    quarter, fourth
cucharita
    teaspoon
cuchara, f -- table-
    spoon
cuchillo, m -- knife
cuenta, f -- bill
cuerda, f -- cord,
    string
cuero, m -- leather
cuidado -- care
cuidadosamente --
    carefully
cultivar -- to
    cultivate
cultivador, m --
    cultivator
curar -- to cure, to
    doctor
curva, f -- curve

D

dar -- to give
dar comida -- feed
de -- of, from
debajo (adv.) --
    under, beneath
decir -- to say,
    tell
dedo, m -- finger
dejar -- to let, to
    leave, to allow
delante (adv.) --
    before, ahead, in
    front of
delantero -- front
demasiado (adv.) --
    too, too much
demasiado (adj.) --
    too much
demasiados (adj.) --
    too many
dentro -- within, in-
    side
deportar -- to deport
deporte, m -- sport
derecho -- right,
    straight
desahijar -- to thin,
    (chop cotton), to
    wean
desahijador, m --
    chopper
descargar -- to un-
    load
descripción, f --
    description
desde -- since, from

desear -- to desire

despedir -- to dismiss, discharge

despertador -- alarm clock

después de (prep.) -- after

después que -- after

detener -- to stop, detain

detrás (adv.) -- behind, after, back

detrás de (prep.) -- behind, after, back

devolver -- to return, pay back

día, m -- day (hoy) -- today

día de fiesta -- holiday

día festivo -- holiday

día de descanso -- day of rest

día de Navidad -- Christmas

día de trabajo -- work day

diario, m -- daily, newspaper

diciembre, m -- December

difícil -- difficult

dinero, m -- money

disco, m -- disk

divisoria -- divisional

doctor -- doctor

dólar -- dollar

doméstico -- domestic

domingo, m -- Sunday

¿dónde? -- where?

¿adónde? -- (to) where?

¿de dónde? -- from where?, of where?

¿en dónde? -- (in) where?

¿para dónde? -- (for) where?

¿por dónde? -- (through) where?

dueño, m -- owner

dulce -- candy

durante -- during

durar -- to last

duro -- hard

E

edad, f -- age

edificio, m -- building

ejote, m -- string beans

embudo, m -- funnel

empacar -- to bale

empacadora, f -- baler

emparejar -- to level land

empleado, m -- employee

empleado (adj.) -- employed

emplear -- to employ

empleo, m -- work, employment

en -- in, or

enchiladas -- enchiladas

93

encendedor -- lighter
encino, m -- oak
encontrar -- to meet,
   find
enero, m -- January
enfermo -- sick
Enrique -- Henry
ensalada, f -- salad
enseñar -- to teach,
   show
enterrar -- to bury
entonces -- then
entrada, f -- entry
   entrance
entrar -- to enter
entre -- between,
   among
entregar -- to hand,
   deliver
envenenar -- to poison
enviar -- to send
envolver -- to wrap,
   bundle
escalera, f -- ladder,
   stairs
escaparse -- to es-
   cape
escoba -- broom
escobar -- to sweep
esconder -- to hide
escribir -- to write
escrito -- written
escritorio -- desk
escuela, f -- school
Español, m -- Spaniard
Español, m -- Spanish
espárrago, m --
   asparagus

especial -- special
espejo, m -- mirror
espinaca, f -- spinach
esposa, f -- wife
esposo, m -- husband
estación, f -- season
   station
estado, m -- state,
   status
Estados Unidos (los
   EE. UU) -- the
   United States
estaño, m -- tin
esta (adj.) -- this
estar -- to be
este, m -- east
este (adj.) -- this
estudiante, m or f --
   student
esweepe, m -- sweep,
   (plow)
examinar -- to examine
excitado -- excited
excusado, m -- toilet
extranjero, m --
   stranger, foreigner

F

fácil -- easy
faja -- girdle
falta -- to lack,
   need
familia, f -- family
febrero, m -- Febru-
   ary
fecha, f-- date (time)
federal, m -- federal,

feliz -- happy
ferrocarril, m --
   railroad
fertilizante, m --
   fertilizer
fertilizar -- to fer-
   tilize
fideo, m -- spaghetti
fijarse en -- to notice
filo, m -- edge
firmar -- to sign
flores, f -- flowers
frazada, f -- blanket
fregador -- dish-
   washer
freno, m -- brakes,
   bridle
fresa -- strawberry
frijoles -- beans
frío, m -- cold (noun)
fritas asadas -- fried
   potatoes
fuego, m -- fire
fuera -- outside
furgón, m -- box car

G

galleta -- cracker
gallina, f -- chicken,
   hen
gallo, m -- rooster
gallipavo -- turkey
ganar -- to earn, win
gancho -- hanger
gas -- gas
gastar -- to spend

gato, f -- cat
gente, f -- people
grampas, f -- staples
grande -- large
grano, m -- grain
gris -- grey
guardarropa -- closet
guarda vaca, f --
   cattle guard
guiar -- to guide,
   drive
gusano, m -- screw
   worm
gustar -- to like,
   please

H

haber -- to have
   (auxiliary)
hablar -- to talk,
   speak
hacendado, m --
   farmer
hacer -- to do, make
hacienda, f -- farm
hacha, f -- ax
hallar, f -- to find
harina, f -- flour
harina de maíz, f--
   corn meal
hasta -- until
hay -- there is, are
helado -- ice cream
helote, m -- roasting
   ear
hembra, f -- female
hermana, f -- sister

95

hermano, m -- brother
hermoso -- pretty,
  beautiful
hierba, f -- grass,
  weed
hígado, m -- liver
hija, f -- daughter
hijo, m -- son
hoja, f -- leaf
higos -- figs
hombre, m -- man
hora, f -- hour
hormiga, f -- ant
hotel, m -- hotel
hoy -- today
hoyo, m -- hole (fence)
huellas, f -- tracks,
  prints
huerta, f -- garden,
  orchard
huevo, m -- egg
húmedo -- damp,
  wet, humid

I

identificación, f --
  identification
iglesia, f -- church
ilegal -- illegal
importante -- impor-
  tant
imposible -- impossible
inglés, m -- English
inglesa, f -- English-
  woman
inmigración, f --
  immigration

inspector, m --
  inspector
insecto, m -- insect
internacional --
  international
invierno, m -- winter
ir -- to go
irse -- to go away
izquierdo -- left

J

jabón -- soap
jamás -- never, ever
jamón, m -- ham
jardín, m -- garden
Jorge -- George
jornalero, m --
  laborer
joven (adj.) -- young
joven, m or f --
  young person
jueves, m -- Thursday
julio, m -- July
junio, m -- June
jurar -- to swear (oath)

L

labor, f -- labor, field
lado, m -- side
ladrillo, m -- brick
lámpara -- lamp
lana, f -- wool
lápiz, m -- pencil
largo -- long
lavamanos -- lavatory
lavar -- to wash

lavarse -- to wash
oneself
lavatorio -- lava-
tory
lección, f -- lesson
leche, f -- milk
lechuga, f -- lettuce
leer -- to read
legal -- legal
legalmente -- legally
legumbres, f -- vege-
tables
lejos -- far
leña, f -- firewood
lentamente -- slowly
lento -- slow
libra, f -- pound
libertar -- to free,
liberate
libre -- free
libro, m -- book
liebre, f -- jack-
rabbit
lija, f -- sandpaper
lima, f -- lime
límite, m -- limit
limón, m -- lemon,
lime
limpio -- clean
lindo -- pretty
línea, f -- line
líquido, m -- liquid
local -- local
lona, f -- canvas,
tarpaulin
llave, f -- wrench, key,
hydrant
lluvia, f -- llover --
rain
lugar, m -- place

lumbre, f -- fire
luminar -- light
luna, f -- moon
lunar, m -- mole
(on person)
lunes, m -- Monday
luz, f -- light
llamar -- to call
llamarse -- to be
named
llanta, f -- tire
llegada, f -- arrival
llegar -- to arrive
llevar -- to carry,
wear

M

macarrones -- macaroni
macho, m -- male
madre, f -- mother
madrugada, f -- dawn,
early morning
maíz, m -- corn
mal -- badly
maleta, f -- suitcase
malo -- bad, sick
mamá -- mamma
mañana, f -- morn-
ing, tomorrow
mancha -- stain, spot
mandar -- to order,
send
manejar -- to drive
mangos -- mangos
mano, f -- hand
manojo, m -- bunch,
bundle
manso -- gentle
mata mosca -- fly
swatter

manteca, f -- lard
mantequilla, f -- butter
manzana, f -- apple
máquina, f -- machine
máquina de escribir --
typewriter
máquinaria, f -- machinary
marcar -- to mark
María -- Mary
marido, m -- husband
marrano (a) -- hog
martes, m -- Tuesday
martillo, m -- hammer
marzo, m -- March
más -- more
mata, f -- stalk
mayo -- May
médico, m -- doctor
medio -- middle, half
mejor -- better
melaza, f -- molasses
melga, f -- plant bed
melocotón -- peach
melón, m -- cantaloupe
menos -- minus, less
mes, m -- month
mesa, f -- table,
plateau
metal, m -- metal
meter -- to put in
mexicano, mejicano --
Mexican
México -- Mexico
mientras -- while
miércoles, m --
Wednesday

miga -- crumb
milla, f -- mile
milpa, f -- maize
land, cornfield
mina, f -- mine
minero, m -- miner
minuto, m -- minute
mirada, f -- glance
mirasol, m -- sun -
flower
molina, f -- mill,
ground feed
montar -- to mount
monte, m -- brush
montura, f -- saddle
morir -- to die
mostaza, f -- mustard
mostrar -- to show
motor, m -- motor
muchacha, f -- girl
muchacho, m -- boy
mucho (adj. or adv.)--
much
muchos (adj.) -- many
muebles, m -- furniture
mujer, f -- woman
mula, f -- mule
muy -- very

N

nabo, m -- turnip
nacer -- to be born
nacimiento, m --
birth
nacionalidad, f --
nationality

nada -- nothing
nadar -- to swim
nadie -- nobody
naranja -- orange
naranja Japonese --
  tangerine
negocio, m --
  business
negro -- black
ni -- neither, nor
ni... no -- neither...
  nor
niara, f -- hay stack
nieve, f -- snow, ice
  cream
ninguno -- none
niño (a) -- child
nivelar -- to level
no -- not, no
noche, f -- night
Nochebuena, f --
  Christmas Eve
nombre, m -- name
norte, m -- north
noviembre, m -- Novem-
  ber
novillo, m -- steer
nueces -- pecan
número, m -- number

O

obtener -- to obtain,
  get
octubre, m -- October
ocupado -- busy
ocurrir -- to occur
oeste, m -- west

ofensa, f -- offence
oficial, m -- officer
oir -- to hear
ojas -- leaves
olla, f -- pot
oro, m -- gold
otoño, m -- autumn
otro -- another
oveja, f -- sheep
ovejero -- shepherd

P

paca, f -- bale
padre -- father
pagar -- to pay
país, m -- country
paja, f -- straw
pijamas -- pajamas
pala, f -- shovel
paleta, f -- ditch
  stopper
palo, m -- stick
paloma, f -- dove
palomitas -- popcorn
pan -- bread
pan tostada -- bread,
  toast
panti medias -- panty
  hose
papá, m -- father,
  papa
papalote, m -- wind-
  mill
para -- for, in order
  to
parar -- to stop
parecer -- to seem,
  appear

pared, f -- wall
parejo, m -- land plane
pasaje, m -- passage
pasar -- to pass
pasar -- to spend (time)
paso, m -- pass, step
pastel, m -- pie
pastilla, f -- cake
pastura, f -- hay
pato, m -- duck
patrón, m -- boss
pecho, m -- chest
pedazo, m -- piece
perder -- to lose
pedir -- to ask for
peine -- comb
película, f -- film
pelo, m -- hair
pelota, f -- ball
pensar -- intend, to think
pepino -- cucumber
peor -- worse
pequeño -- small
pera, f -- pear
peral, m -- pear tree
perdices, m -- partridges
perejil, m -- parsley
perezoso -- lazy
periódico, m -- newspaper
permiso, m -- permit permission
pero -- but

persona, f -- person
pesar -- to weigh
peso, m -- dollar (Mexican)
petróleo, m -- petroleum, oil
pie, m -- foot
piel, f -- skin, hide
pico, m -- chisel, pick
pimiento, m -- black pepper
pimentero -- pepper shaker
pina -- pineapple
pintura -- picture
pinzas, f -- pincers
pipa, f -- pipe
piscador, m -- picker
piscar -- to pick
pistola, f -- pistol
planchar -- to iron, press
plantar -- to plant
plata, f -- silver
plátano -- banana
platicar -- to chat
plato, m -- plate, dish
plaza, f -- plaza, square
pluma, f -- pen
pobre -- poor
poco (adj.) -- little
pocos (adj.) -- few

poder -- to be able, can
pollo, m -- chicken,
  fryer
polvo, m -- powder
poner -- to put, place
ponerse -- to put on
por -- for, through,
  by
por eso -- for that
  reason
porqué -- because
¿porque? -- why?
posible -- possible
potrero, m -- trap
potro, m -- colt
preparar -- to prepare
presentar -- to present
primavera, f -- spring
primo (a) -- cousin
promesa, f -- promise
prometer -- to pro-
  mise
próximo -- next
prueba, f -- proof
pueblo, m -- town,
  people
puente, m -- bridge
puerco, m -- hog
puerta, f -- door
puerto, m -- port
pulga, f -- flea
pulgada, f -- inch
pulgar, m -- thumb
punta, f -- point

¿qué? -- what?
que -- that
que -- than
¿quién? -- who?
¿a quién? -- whom?
¿de quien? -- whose?
quedar (se) -- stay,
  to remain
quelite, m -- care-
  less weed
querer -- to wish,
  want
queso, m -- cheese
quitar -- to take off

R

rábano, m -- radish
rabo, m -- top
  (plants)
raíces -- roots
ramas -- limbs
rápidamente --
  rapidly
rápido -- rapid,
  fast
ranchero, m --
  rancher
rancho, m -- ranch,
  farm
repollo chiquito, m --
  brussel sprouts
rastrear -- to rake,
  to harrow

101

rastrillo, m -- rake
rata, f -- rat
ratito, m -- very
   short time
rato, m -- short
   time
ratón, m -- mouse
rayado -- striped
recibir -- to receive
recibo, m -- receipt
record -- record
regación, f --
   irrigation
regadora, f --
   sprayer
regar -- to irri-
   gate
registrar -- to
   search, register
regresar -- to return
renta, f -- rent
rentar -- to rent
reparar -- to
   repair, to fix
repisas -- shelves
repollo, m -- cabbage
regadero -- sprinkler
resol -- baking pow-
   der
retrato, m -- picture
reunir -- to unite,
   join
revolver, m -- re-
   volver (noun)
rico -- rich
riego, m -- irrigation
río, m -- river

riñon, m -- kidney
rojo -- red
romana, f -- scales
ropa, f -- clothing
rueda, f -- wheel

S

sábana, f -- sheet
sábado, m -- Satur-
   day
saber -- to know (how)
sacar -- to take out
sacate, m -- grass,
   hay
sal, m -- salt
sala -- living room
salchichas, f --
   sausage
salida, f --
   departure
salir -- to leave,
   depart
salmón -- salmon
salud, f -- health
sandalias -- house-
   shoes
sardina, m -- sar-
   dine
seco, m -- dry
seda, f -- silk
según -- according to
seguro -- certain,
   sure, safe
semana, f -- week
sendero, m -- path,
   trail

102

sentado -- seated
sentarse -- to sit
  down
sentir -- to feel
Señor, m -- Mr., sir
Señora, f -- Mrs.,
  lady
Señorita -- Miss,
  young lady
sepultar -- to bury
serrucho, m -- saw
si -- if
sí -- yes
siempre -- always
siglo, m -- century
signo, m -- sign
silla, f -- chair
sillón -- arm chair
silvestre -- wild
sin -- without
sino -- but, only,
  except
sitio, m -- site,
  place
sofá, f -- sofa
solicitar -- induce,
  to solicit
solo -- alone
solo -- only
sombrero, m -- hat
subir -- to climb
suegra, f -- mother-
  in-law
suegro, m -- father-
  in-law
suerte, f -- luck
sur, m -- south
surco, m -- row
sweater -- sweter

T

tacos -- tacos
tallo, m -- stalk
también -- as well,
  also, too
tampoco -- neither,
  not either
tan -- as, so
tanque, m -- tank
tanto -- as much
tantos -- as many
tapar -- to stop up
tapas, f -- tops
tarde, f -- afternoon
tarde -- late
tarjeta, f -- card
taxi, m -- taxi
taza, f -- cup
te -- tea
teatro, m -- theater
Tejas -- Texas
tejón, m -- raccoon
teléfono, m --
  telephone
telefonear -- to
  telephone
televisión -- tele-
  vision
temprano -- early
tener -- to have,
  possess
tenedor, m -- fork
tequila, m -- tequila
tiempo, m -- time,
  weather
tienda, f -- store
tijeras -- clippers
tinta, f -- ink
tía, f -- aunt
tío, m -- uncle

tirar -- to pull,
  shoot
toalla -- towel
tocino, m -- bacon
todavía -- yet still
todavía no -- not yet
todo -- all
todo el mundo --
  everybody
tomate, m -- tomato
tomar -- to take,
  drink
Tomás -- Thomas
toro, m -- bull
tornillo, f -- screw
toronja, f --
  grapefruit
tortillas -- tortillas
trabajar -- to work
trabajo, m -- work
traer -- to bring
traje -- dress
traje, m -- suit
  (clothes)
trasquilar -- to shear
tren, m -- train
trigo, m wheat
trillar -- to thrash
trilladora, f --
  harvester, thrasher
tripas, f -- entrails
triste -- sad
troncidores, m -- cut
  worms
tronco -- trunk tree
troquero, m -- trucker
tubo, m -- tube, pipe

U

ubre -- teat,
  udder
últimamente -- lately,
  lastly
último -- last
una, f -- fingernail,
  claw
útil -- useful
uva, f -- grape

V

vaca, f -- cow
vagón, m -- wagon
valer -- to be worth
válido -- valid
vapor, m -- steam,
  ship
vaquero, m -- cow-
  boy
varios (as) --
  several, various
vaso, m -- glass
vasija, f -- dishes
venado, m -- deer
vecino (a) -- neighbor
vender -- to sell
veneno, m -- poison
venida, f -- arrival,
  coming
venir -- to come
ventana, f -- window
ver -- to see
verano, m -- summer
verdad, f -- truth,
  true
verde -- green

verduras, f -- green
  vegetables
verenja, f -- egg
  plant
vestido, m -- dress
vestir (se) -- to
  dress
vez, f -- time
  (numerically)
viajar -- to travel
viaje, m -- journey,
  ,trip
vibora, f -- rattle-
  snake
viejo -- old, old
  person
viernes, f -- Friday
vino, m -- wine
visa, f - - visa
visita, f -- visit
vivir -- to live
volante -- flying

Z

zanahorias, f --
  carrots
zapatería, f --
  shoe shop
zapatero, m --
  cobbler
zapato, m -- shoe
zorro, m -- fox

Y

y -- and
ya -- already
yarda, m or f --
  yard
yegua, f - - mare
yo -- I

CHAPTER XXV

ENGLISH--SPANISH VOCABULARY

A

a -- un, una
abandon -- dejar, abandonar
able -- poder
about -- acera de como
above -- sobre, encima, arriba
absence -- ausencia, f
absent -- ausente
abuse -- maltratar
accept -- aceptar
accident -- accidente, m
accompany -- acompañar
accord -- acuerdo, m
according to -- según
accuse -- acusar
ache -- dolor, m; doler
acquaintance -- conocido
acre -- acre, m
across -- a traves de
address -- dirección, f
admission -- admisión, f
admit -- admitir
adopt -- adoptar
advice -- aviso, m; consejo, m
advise -- avisar; aconsejar
affair -- asunto, m; negocio, m

affidavit -- declaración, f
afoot -- a pie
afraid -- miedo, m
after -- después (de) (que)
afternoon -- tarde, f
afterwards -- después
again -- otra vez; de nuevo
age -- edad, f
agent -- agente, m
agree -- convenir; estar conforme
agreement -- acuerdo, m; pacto, m
air -- aire, m
alarm clock -- despertador
alfalfa -- alfalfa, f
alien -- extranjero, m; ajeno, m
alive -- vivo, m
all -- todo
alley -- callejón, m
allow -- permitir; dejar
almond -- almendra, f
almost -- casi
alone -- solo
along -- a largo de
already -- ya
also -- también
although -- aunque

always -- siempre
America -- América, f
American -- americano
among -- entre
an -- un, una
and -- y
andiron -- mortillo, m
angry -- enojado
animal -- animal, m
Annie -- Anita
another -- otro
answer -- contestar;
  responder
ant -- hormiga, f
ant bed -- hormiguero, m
antique -- antiguo, m
any -- alguno
anybody -- alguien
anything -- alguna
  cosa; algo
apartment -- apartamiento,
  m
appear -- aparecer;
  parecer
appetite -- apetito, m
apple -- manzana, f
apple sauce -- compota
  de manzanas, f
application -- aplicación,
  f
apply -- solicitar,
  aplicar

appointment -- compro-
  miso, m; cita, f
apprehend -- prender;
  aprenhender; arrestar,
  agarrar
approach -- acercarse a
apricot -- albaricoque
April -- abril
apron -- delantal, m
area -- área
argue -- disputar; arguir
arm -- brazo, m; arma, f
arm chair -- sillón
army -- ejército, m
around -- alrededor
arrange -- arreglar
arrangements -- arreg-
  los, m
arrest -- aprehender;
  arrestar; arresto, m
arrival -- llegada, f;
  venida, f
arrive -- llegar
archive -- archivo, m
art -- arte, m
Arthur -- Arturo
article -- artículo, m
artist -- artista, m
as -- como
as....as -- tan....como
as much...as -- tanto...
  como

as many...as -- tantos...
como
asbestos -- asbesto;
amianto, m
ash tray -- cenicero
ask (question) -- pre-
guntar
ask for -- pedir
asparagus -- espárrago,
m
assault -- asaltar;
asalto, m
assist -- ayudar;
asistar
assistant -- ayudante,
m
asthma -- asma, f
at -- a, en
at last -- finalmente;
al fin, por fin
at least -- por lo menos;
al menos; a lo menos
at once -- al instante;
en seguida
at present -- actualmente
attack -- ataque, m
attend -- prestar atención
attic -- ático, m
August -- agosto, m
aunt -- tía, f
authorize -- autorizar
automobile -- coche, m;
automovil, m; carro, m

autumn -- otoño, m
avocado -- aguacate
avenue -- avenida, f
await -- aguardar
awake -- despertar
away -- lejos
awning -- toldo, m
ax -- hacha, m

B

baby -- niño (a); bebi;
nene, m; nena, f;
infante, m
bachelor -- soltero, m
back -- espalda, f; atrás;
detrás
backbone -- espinazo, m
back-door -- puerta
trasera, f
back of -- detras de
back-seat -- asiento
trasero, m
bacon -- tocino, m
bad -- malo
badge -- insignia, f;
placa, f
badly -- mal
bag -- saco, m
baggage -- equipaje, m
bail -- fianza, f
bait -- carnado, m
bake -- cocer; asar
baker -- panadero, m

bakery -- panadería, f
baking powder -- resol, m
bald -- calvo; pelón
bale -- paca; bala;
   empacar
baler -- empacadora, f
ball -- pelota, f; bola, f
bamboo -- bambú, m
banana -- plátano
bandage -- vendaje, m
bank -- barranca, f;
   banco, m; orilla, f
banker -- banquero, m
baptize -- bautizar
baptismal certificate --
   fe de bautismo
bar -- cantina, f
barbed wire -- alambre
   de pico
barbeque -- barbacoa
barber -- peluquero, m;
   barbero, m
barber shop -- barbería,
   f; peluquería, f
barefoot -- descalzo, m
bark -- (of tree) corteza,
   f
barn -- granero, m
barrel -- barril, m
bartender -- cantinero, m
basket -- canasta, f
basket -- (large)
   canasto, m

baste -- (meat) enlardar
bath -- baño, m
bathe -- bañarse
battery -- batería, f
be -- ser, estar
be able -- poder
be acquainted with --
   conocer
be born -- nacer
be named -- llamarse
be pleasing to -- gustar
be worth -- valer
beach -- playa, f
bead -- cuenta, f
beans -- frijoles, m
beans -- (string) ejote, m
beard -- barba, f
beat -- batido, m
beater -- batido , m
beautiful -- hermoso;
   lindo; bello
because -- porque
because of -- a cause de;
   por
bed -- cama, f
bedpan -- silleta, f
bedroll -- mochila, f;
   tendido, m
bedspread -- sobrecama, f
bee -- abeja, f
bee-hive -- colmena, f
beef steak -- biftec, m
beer -- cerveza, f

beetle -- escarabajo, m
beets -- betabeles, m
before (time) -- antes de
before (front of) -- delante
de
begger -- mendigo, m;
limosnero, m
begin -- empezar,
comenzar; principiar
behave -- portarse
behind -- atrás; detrás
beige -- beige; color
arena, m
belch -- eructo, m
believe -- creer
believe in -- aprobar
bell -- campaña, f
belly -- panzón, m; panza,
f
belong to -- pertenecer
below -- debajo de;
abajo; bajo
belt -- cinto, m; cintura,
f
beneath -- debajo; bajo
bench -- banco, m
bend -- encorvar
bent -- talento, m
berry -- baya, f
best -- el mejor
better -- mejor
between -- entre
bib -- babero, m
Bible -- Biblia, f

bicycle -- bicicleta, f
big -- grande
bigamist -- bígamo, m
bigamy -- bigamia, f
bill -- cuenta, f
binocular -- binocular, m
bird -- pájaro, m
birth -- nacimiento, m
birth certificate -- cer-
tificado de
nacimiento, m
birthday -- cumpleaños,
birth mark -- marca de
nacimiento
biscuit -- bisquetes;
bizcocho
bit -- pedazo, m
black -- negro
blackberry -- zarza, f
blackish -- prieto
blame -- culpa, f
blanket -- cobija, f;
frazada, f
bleach -- lejía, f
blind -- ciego
block -- bloque, m;
cuadra, f; soquete, m
block -- manzana, f
blond -- huero; rubio
blood -- sangre, f
bloom -- flor, f
blouse -- blusa, f
blue -- azul

boat -- bote, m; buque,
m; barco, m
boat (row) -- chalupa, f
body -- cuerpo, m
boil -- cocer; hervir
bolt -- cerrojo, m
bond (bail) -- fianza, f
bone -- hueso, m
bonnet -- capota
book -- libro, m
bookcase -- amario de
libros
boot -- bota, f
border -- frontera
Border Patrol -- Patrula
de la Frontera; Pa-
trulla Fronteriza
born -- nacer; nacido
borrow -- pedir pres-
tado
boss -- patrón, m; jefe,
m; mayordomo, m
boss (main) -- mero
gallo
both -- ambos, los dos
bottle -- botella, f
bottom -- base, m
bowl -- cazuela
box -- caja, f; cajón, m
boy -- muchacho, m
bracelet -- pulsera, f
brakes -- frenos, m
branch -- rama, f
brass -- latón, m

brassiere -- brasier
brawl -- barulla, f;
disputa, f
bread -- pan, m
bread -- pan tostada
break into -- escalar
break -- quebrar; romper
breakfast -- desayunar;
desayuno, m
breast -- pecho, m
brewery -- cervecería, f
brick -- ladrillo, m
bricklayer -- albañil, m;
ladrillero, m
bridge -- puente, m or f
bridle -- freno, m
bring -- traer
broad -- ancho
broccoli -- bróculi, m
broil -- asar empanizar
broken -- roto; quebrado
bronze -- bronce, m
broom -- escoba, f
broth -- caldo, m
brother -- hermano
brother-in-law -- cuñado,
m
brown -- café; pardo;
moreno
brunette -- moreno;
trigueno
brush -- cepillo, m;
cepillar
brush -- matorral, m

brussel sprouts --
repollo chiquito, m
bucket -- balde, m;
bote, m
bug -- chinche, f
build -- construir
building -- edificio, m
bulb -- bulbo, m
bull -- toro, m
bullet -- balazo, m; bala, f
bunch -- manojo, m;
bunche, m
bundle -- paquete, m;
bulto, m
burn -- quemadura, f
burro -- burro, m
bury -- sepultar;
enterrar
bus -- camíon, m; bus, m;
exteche, m; omnibus, m
business -- negocio, m;
asunto, m
busy -- ocupado
but -- pero; sino; más
butcher -- carnicero, m
butcher shop -- carni-
cería, f
butter -- mantequilla, f
button -- botón, m
buttonhole -- ojal, m
buy -- comprar
by -- por
by (near) -- cerca

by means of -- por
medio de

C

cabbage -- repollo, m;
col, m
cabinet -- gabinete
cactus -- nopal
cafe -- café, m
cage -- (bird's, ani-
mal's) jaula, f
cake -- pastilla, f
calendar -- calendario, m
calf -- becerro, m;
ternero, m
call -- llamar
camera -- máquina
fotográfica, f
can -- lata, f; bote, m
can -- (to be able) poder
can milk -- leche latada
can opener -- abre latas
candle -- vela, f
candlestick -- candelero,
m
candy -- dulce
canoe -- canoa, f;
chalupa, f
canteloupe -- melón, f
canvas -- lona, f
cap -- cachucha, f; gorra,
f
cape -- capa, f

capital -- capital, f
capsule -- cápsula, f
car -- carro, m; auto, m;
coche, m; máquina, f;
automovil, m
car (box) -- furgón, m
car jack -- yaque, m;
gato, m
caramel -- caramelo, m
carburetor -- carburador,
m
card -- tarjeta, f
care (to take) -- cuidar
care -- cuidado, m
carefully -- cuidadosa-
mente
careless weed -- quelite,
m
carpenter -- carpintero, f
carpenter shop -- car-
pintería, f
carpet -- alfombra, f
carrots -- zanahorias, f
carry -- llevar
casement windows --
ventana, f
cash -- al contado
cashew -- (nut) anacardo,
m
cashier -- cajero, m;
contador, m
cashmere -- cachemira, f
castrate -- capar
cat -- gato, m

cat food -- comida al
gato
catch -- agarrar; coger
caterpillar -- oruga, f
catfish -- vaigre, m
cattle -- ganado, m
cattle guard -- guarda
vaca, f
cattleman -- ganadero, m
cause -- causa, f;
causar
cauliflower -- coliflor, m
cave -- cueva, f
cayenne pepper -- pimen-
tón, m
celery -- apio, m
cement -- cemento, m
cemetery -- cementerio,
m; panteon, m
cent -- centavo, m
century -- siglo, m
cereal -- cereal, m
certain -- cierto; seguro
certainly -- ciertamente,
¿como no?
certificate -- certificado,
m
certify -- afimar;
certificar
chain -- cadena, f
chair -- silla, f
chair, rocking -- silla,
mecedora
chalk -- tiza, f

chance -- chanza, f;
oportunidad, f
chandelier -- araña de
luces, f
change -- cambriar;
cambio, m; mudar
chaps -- chapaderas, f
charcoal -- carbón de
leña, m
Charles -- Carlos
charming -- simpático
chat -- platicar; charlar
chaffeur -- chofer, m
cheap -- barato
check -- revisar; checar
check -- (commercial)
cheque, m
cheek -- mejilla, f
cheese -- queso, m
cherry -- ciruela, f;
cereza
chest -- pecho, m
chewing gum -- chicle

chicken -- gallina, f
(fried) pollo
al horno
chief -- jefe, m
chiffon -- chifón, m
child -- niño (a); cha-
maco (a); criatura, f
children -- niños, m
chile -- chile
chin -- barbilla, f; barba, f

china -- porcelana, f
chisel -- pico, m
chocolate -- chocolate
chop -- (mince) picar
Christmas -- Navidad, f;
Natividad, f
Christmas Eve -- Noche-
buena, f
church -- iglesia, f
chute -- shute, m
cigar -- puro, m
cigarette -- cigarro, m;
cigarrillo, m
circus -- circo
citizen -- ciudadano (a)
citizenship -- ciudada-
nia, f
city -- ciudad, f
civil -- civil
class -- clase, f
clean -- limpiar, limpio
clear -- claro
clearly, -- claramente
clerk -- dependiente, m
climb -- subir
clippers -- tijeras
clock -- reloj, m
clod -- (dirt) terrón, m
clorox -- cloralex
close -- cerrar
close to -- cerca de
closed -- cerrado
closet -- gabinete, m

cloth -- tela, f
clothes -- vestidos, m;
  ropa, f;
  (dryer) secadora de
  ropa
  (closet) guardarropa
cloud -- nube, f
coal -- carbón, m
coat -- abrirgo
  saco, m
cobbler -- zapatero, m
cobweb -- telaraña, f
cocktail -- cótel, coctel,
  m
cocoa -- cacao, m
coconut -- coco
coffee -- café, m
  (c. pot) -- cafetera
  (c. Table) -- cafeto
cold -- frío (adj.); frío,
  m; resfriado, m
collar -- cuello, m
collect -- cobrar
collide -- chocar
collision -- choque, m
colony -- colonia, f
color -- color, m
colt -- potro, m
comb -- peine
come -- venir
commit -- cometer
communist -- comunista
companion -- compañero,
  m

company -- compañía, f
compartment -- com-
  partimiento, m
complete -- completar;
  acabar; terminar;
  completo (adj.)
comply -- cumplir
concerning -- tocante (a);
  respecto (a); acerca
  de; en cuanto (a)
concrete -- concreto, m
condemn -- condenar
conduct -- condenar
confess -- confesar
consent -- consentir
constable -- alguacil, m
construct -- construir
consul -- cónsul, m
contain -- contener;
  caber
contented -- contento
contents -- contenidos, m
continue -- continuar
contract -- contracto, m
contract laborer --
  bracero, m
contractor -- contratista,
  m
converse -- conversar
convict -- condenar;
  convicto, m
cook -- cocinar;
  cocinero, m

115

cool -- fresco
cop -- chote, m; jura, m
copper -- cobre, m
(c. vessel) caldera, f
cord -- cuerda, f; cordón, m
core -- (of a fruit) corazón, m
cork -- corcho
(c. of a bottle) tapón
(c. screw) sacacorchos, m
corn -- (fresh) helote
(c. dry in sack) maíz, m
corner -- (inside) rincón, (outside) esquina, f
cornfield -- milpa, f
corral -- corral, m
correct -- correcto; corregir
cost -- costar
cotton -- algodón, m
couch -- sofá, m
counsel -- consejo, m; aconsejar
count -- contar
country -- (outside city) campo, m
(nation) país, m
(fatherland) patria, f
countryman -- campesino, m

countryman -- (fellow) paisano, m
county -- condado, m
court -- tribunal, m; corte, f; juzgado, m
cousin -- primo (a)
cover -- cubrir
coveralls -- overoles, m
covered -- cubierto
cow -- vaca, f
cowboy -- vaquero, m
crab -- cangrejo, m
crack -- (muts) cascar
cracker -- galleta
crawl -- arrastrarse
crayfish -- cangrejo de río
crayon -- carbón, m
crazy -- loco
cream -- crema, f
(whipped c.) nata batida, f
crease -- (wrinkle) arruga, f
credit -- crédito, m
creek -- arroyo, m; riachuelo, m
crime -- crimen, m; delito, m
criminal -- criminal, m; reo, m
crippled -- cojo

crisp -- crespo, m
crochet -- ganchilli, m
cross -- cruzar; cruz, f
crumb -- miga, f
crust -- (of bread, pie)
corteza, f
cry -- llorar; gritar;
grito, m
cube -- cubo, m
cucumber -- cohombro, m
cuff -- (of sleeve) puño, m
cuff links -- gemelos, m
cultivate -- cultivar
cultivator -- cultivador,
m
cup -- taza, f
cupful -- taza, f
curl -- (of hair) rizo
curtains -- cortinas, f
customhouse -- aduana, f
custom inspector -- adu-
anero, m; inspector de
aduana
curve -- curva, f
cushion -- almohada, f
custard -- flan, m
cut -- cortada, f; cortar

(c. worms) tronci-
dores, m

D
dad -- papá, m
daffodil -- narciso
trompón, m

daily -- diario
dairy -- lechería, f
dam -- presa, f
damage -- daño, m; danar
damask -- (cloth)
damasco, m
dance -- bailar; baile, m
dandruff -- caspa, f
danger -- peligro, m
dark -- obscuro; moreno,
prieto, trigueño
(to become d.) obscure-
cerse
date -- fechar; fecha, f;
compromiso; cita, m
daughter -- hija, f
daughter-in-law -- nuera,
f
dawn -- amanecer, m;
madrugada, f
day -- día, m
(d. before yesterday)
anteayer
(d. after tomorrow)
pasado mañana
(d. of rest) día de
descanso
dead -- muerto
deaf -- sordo
dear -- (affection) querido
(costly) caro
death -- muerte, f

debt -- deuda, f
deceive -- engañar
December -- diciembre, m
decide -- decidir
declare -- declarar
decoration -- decoración, f
deed -- hecho, m; acto, m
deep -- hondo
deep freeze -- hielera
deer -- venado, m
defect -- defecto, m
defendant -- acusado, m
delicious -- delicioso
deliver -- entregar
demand -- demandar; demanda, f
den -- (study) gabinete, m
dentist -- dentista, m
deny -- negar
deodorant -- desodorante, m
depart -- partir; salir
departure -- partida, f; salida, f
depend -- depender
dependent -- dependiente, m
deportation -- deportación, f
deported -- deportado

describe -- describir
description -- descripción, f
desert dishes -- copas
dessert -- postre, m; flan
desire -- desear; deseo, m
desk -- mesa, f; escritorio
destination -- destinación, f
detail -- detalle, m
detective -- detective, m; dectectivo, m
dew -- rocio
diabetes -- diabetes,m
diaper -- (baby's) pañal, m
die -- morir
difference -- diferencia, f
different -- deferente
difficult -- dificil
dine -- (at midday) comer (in evening) cenar
dining room -- mesa del comedor, m
dinner -- (midday) comida, f (evening) cena, f
dip -- immersión, f
dirt -- polvo, m; tierra, f
dirty -- cochino; sucio

118

dish -- (food) plato;
   (meat, fruit, etc.)
   fuente, m
dishes -- vasija; trastos,
   m
dishwasher -- fregador
disinfect -- desinfectar
dismiss -- despedir
dismiss -- (fire) deso-
   cupar; despedir
disorder -- desorden, m
dispute -- mitote, m;
   disputa, f
distance -- distancia, f
distant -- distante
district -- barrio, m;
   distrito, m
ditch -- zanja, f; diche,
   m; canal, m; acequia, f
dive -- buceo, m
divide -- dividir
divorce -- divorciar;
   divorcio, m
do -- hacer
doctor -- médico, m;
   doctor, m
doctor -- (to heal, cure)
   curar
document -- documento, m
doe -- gama, f
dog -- perro, m
doll -- muñeca, f
dollar -- dólar, m;
   peso, m

domestic -- doméstico
donkey -- asno, m; burro,
   m
door -- puerta, f
double -- doble; doblar
doubt -- dudar; duda, f
dove -- paloma, f
down -- abajo; bajo
down -- (get down)
   bajarse de
dozen -- docena, f
drain -- desaguadero, m
drapery -- colgaduras, f
drawer -- comada, f
dress -- (with clothes)
   vestirse
   (d. suit) traje, m
dresser -- cómoda
dressmaker -- modista, f
dried -- seco
   (of fruit) paso, m
drink -- beber; tomar;
   trago, m
drive -- manejar; guiar
driver -- chofer, m
driver's license --
   licencia de manejar
drop -- gota, f
drug -- droga, f
druggist --droguero,
   m; boticario
drug store -- botica f;
   farmacía, f; droguería,

119

drunk -- borracho; ebrio;
tomado
drunkard -- borrachón, m
dry -- secar; seco;
árrido
duck -- pato, m
dump -- dumpe, m
during -- durante
dust -- polvo, m
duty -- deber, m; obli-
gación, f
duties (custom) --
derechos

E

each -- cada; todo
eagle -- el águila, f
ear -- (inner) oído, m
(outer) oreja, f
early -- temprano
earn -- ganar
earring -- arete
earth -- tierra, f
easily -- fácilmente
east -- este, m; oriente,
m
easy -- fácil
eat -- comer
(e. breakfast)
desayunarse
(e. supper) cenar
edge -- bordo, m
Edward -- Eduardo

egg -- huevo, m
(fried e.) huevo
frito, m
(boiled e.) huevo
cocido, m
(poached e.) huevo
escalfado, m
(scrambled e.)
huevo revueltos,
m
(with tomato, pep-
per, etc.)
ranchero, m
eggplant -- verenja, f
eight -- ocho
eighteen -- diez y ocho
eighth -- octavo
eighty -- ochenta
either -- o
either -- ... uno u otro
elastic -- elástico, m
(e. band) anillo de
gama, m
elbow -- codo, m
electric -- eléctrico
electricity -- electricidad,
f
elegant -- elegante
elephant -- elefante, m
eleven -- once
elk -- ante, m
elm -- olmo, m
embark -- embarcar

embroidery -- bordado, m
emigrant -- emigrante, m
employ -- emplear; dar
 empleo; ocupar
employed -- empleado
employee -- empleado, m
employer -- patrón, m;
 mayordomo, m
employment -- empleo, m
empty -- vacío
enchiladas -- enchiladas
end -- acabar; terminar
enema -- lavativa, f
engine -- locomotora,
 f; máquina, f
engineer -- ingeniero, m;
 maquinista, m
English -- inglés, m
English -- (adj.) inglés (a)
enough -- bastante;
 suficiente
enter -- entrar; pasar
entertain -- divertir
envelope -- sobre, m
epsom salts -- sal de la
 higuera, f
equal -- igual
ermine -- armiño, m
errand -- mandado, m;
 recado, m
error -- error, m; falta, f
especial -- especial
Europe -- Europa
even -- llano; liso

evening -- tarde, f
ever -- jamás, alguna vez;
 siempre
every -- cada; todos
everybody -- todo el
 mundo
everything-- todo; todo
 lo que
everywhere -- por todas
 partes
evidence -- evidencia, f
exact -- exacto; mero
exactly -- exactamente;
 mero
examination -- examen, m
examine -- examinar;
 revisar; inspeccionar;
 registrar
example -- ejemplo, m
excellent -- excelente
exclude -- excluir; negar
 la entrada
exclusion -- exclusión, f
excuse -- dispensar;
 excusar; excusa, f
exercise -- ejercicio, m
expect -- esperar
expense -- gasto, m;
 coste, m
explain -- explicar
export -- exportar
express -- expresar;
 manifestar; expreso,
 m; expres, m

121

extend -- extender
extension -- extensión, f
extra -- extra
eye -- ojo, m
   (e. brow) ceja, f
   (e. lash) pestaña, f
   (e. lid) párpado, m
eyeglasses -- lentes, m;
   anteojos, m

F

face -- cara, f
fact -- hecho, m
fair -- claro, m
faith -- fe, f
fall -- caer
false -- falso
falsehood -- falsedad, f
family -- familia, f
fan -- abanico
far -- (away) lejos
far -- (from) lejos de
fare -- pasaje, m
farm -- hacienda, f;
   rancho, m
farmer -- hacendado, m;
   agricultor, m;
   ranchero, m
farm laborer -- labrador,
   m; cultivador, m;
   sembrador, m
farther -- mas lejos
fast -- recio; aprisa;
   rapido

fat -- gordo; grueso
father -- padre, m;
   papá, m
father-in-law -- suegro,
   m
fault -- falta, m; culpa, f
fear -- temer; tener
   miedo, m; temore, m
February -- febrero, m
federal -- federal
fee -- derecho, m
feed -- alimento, m
feel -- sentir (se); tocar
felt -- fieltro, m
female -- hembra
fence -- cerca, f
fern -- helecho, m
fertilize -- fertilizar;
   abonar
fertilizer -- abone, m;
   fertilizante, m
fever -- fiebre, m
few -- pocos
fewer -- menos
fifteen -- quince
fifth -- quinto
fifty -- cincuenta
fight -- pelear; pelea, f;
   combatir, f; combate, m
figs -- higos
file -- (tool) lima, f
   (smooth) limar
   (for letters, bills)
   archivo, m

file charges -- poner una
   queja
fill -- llenar
fillet -- (of meat or
   fish) filete, m
filling -- (of tooth)
   empastadura, f
filling station -- depósito
   de gasolina, m
filly -- jaca, potra, f
film -- película, f
final -- final
finally -- al fin;
   finalmente
find -- encontrar; hallar
   (to find out) saber;
   averiguar
fine -- (good) bueno, fino
fine -- imponer una multa;
   multar; multa, f
finger -- dedo, m
fingernail -- uña, f
fire -- fuego, m; lumbre,
   m
   (f. a gun) tirar;
   disparar
   (to dismiss)
   desocupar
fireman -- bombero, m;
   fogonero, m
fireplace -- hogar, m;
   chimenea, f
first -- primero

fish -- pez, m; pescado;
   pescar
fisherman -- pescador, m
fit -- adjustar
   (of a garment) corte,
   m
five -- cinco
five hundred --
   quinientos
fix -- arreglar; reparar;
   componer
flag -- bandera, f
flake -- escama, f
flaky -- escamoso
flat -- ponchada, f; flat,
   m; pinchada, f
flea -- pulga, f
flood -- inundación, f;
   diluvio, m
floor -- suelo, m; piso, m
flower -- flor, f
   (f. bed) almárciga
   (f. pot) maceta
flue -- cañón, m
fly -- (insect) mosca, f
fly swatter -- matamosca
fly -- (to fly) volvar
foil -- papel aluminio
fold -- doblez, f
follow -- seguir
food -- comida, f
fool -- tonto (a)

123

foot -- pie, m;
　(of animals, furni-
　ture) pata, f
　(of bed, page, etc.)
　pie, m
foot bridge -- tabla, f;
　puente de a pie
foot path -- senda (de pie)
for -- para; por
force -- fuerza, f
forearm -- antebrazo, m
forehead -- frente, f
foreigner -- extranjero
　(a)
foreman -- mayordomo,
　m; patrón, m;
　rallador, m
forest -- selva, f; bosque,
　m
forgery -- falsificación, f
forget -- olvidar
fork -- tenedor, m;
　horca, f
former -- (previous)
　anterior
former -- aquel
forty -- cuarenta
forward -- adelante;
　delante
fountain pen -- pluma
　fuente
fountain -- (water) fuente
　de agua

four -- cuatro
fourth -- cuarto
fourteen -- catorce
fox -- zorro, m
Frank -- Pancho; Fran-
　cisco
free -- libre; libertar;
　librar
freeze -- helar
French -- francés
frequently -- frecuente-
　mente, a menudo
fresh -- fresco
friar -- fraile, m
Friday -- viernes, m
fried -- frito
friend -- amigo (a)
friend (close) --
　compadre, m
from -- de; desde
front -- frente; delantero
front of -- delante de
frozen -- helado, m
fruit -- fruta, f
fry -- fritada, f
frying -- fritura, f
frying pan -- sartén, m
fryer -- pollo
fulfill -- cumplir
full -- lleno
fun -- diversión, f

furniture -- muebles, m
(f. store)
mueblería, f
(outdoor f.) muebles
de patio
future -- futuro, m;
porvenir, m

G

gain -- ganar
gallon -- galón, m
game -- juego, m
gap -- boquilla, f
garage -- garage, m;
garaje, m
garden -- jardín, m;
huerta, f
gardener -- jardinero, m
garlic -- ajo, m
garments -- ropa, f;
vestidos, m; prendas
de vestir
garter -- liga, f
(g. belt) liga, f
gas -- gas, m
gasoline -- gasolina, f
gate -- puerta, f;
entrada, f
(entrance g.)
garita, f
gather -- piscar; coger
gelatine -- gelatina, f
generally -- generalmente

gentle -- manso
gentleman -- caballero,
m; señor, m
George -- Jorge
German -- alemán, m
Germany -- Alemania
get -- obtener; conse-
guir; sacar
get -- (into vehicle)
subir (se) a
get -- (out or off a
vehicle) bajar (se) de
get up -- levantarse
giblets -- menudillos, m
gin -- (drink) ginebra, f
ginger -- jengibre, m
gingham -- guinga, f
girdle -- faja
girl -- muchacha, f;
niña, f
give -- dar
gizzard -- molleja, f
gladiolus -- gladíolo,
gladio, m; espadaña, f
glance -- mirada, f;
ojeada, f
glass -- vidrio, m
(drinking g.) vaso
glove -- guante, m
go -- ir
(depart) irse
goat -- chivo, m; cabra, f
God -- Dios

125

godchild -- ahijado (da)
goddaughter -- ahijada, f
godfather -- padrino, m
godmother -- madrina, f
godson -- ahijado, m
gold -- oro, m
goldfish -- carpa dorada, f
good -- bueno
  (g. afternoon) buenas
    tardes
  (g.bye) adios; hasta
    luego, hasta la
    vista
  (g.morning) buenos
    días
  (g.night) buenas
    noches
government -- gobierno,
  m
gown -- toga, f
grade -- grado, m
grain -- grano, m
granddaughter -- nieta, f
  (g. father) abuelo, m
  (g. mother) abuela, f
  (g. son) nieto, m
grape -- uva, f
grapefruit -- toronja, f
grasp -- agarrar
grass -- sacate, m;
  hierba, f
grater -- rallador, m

grave yard -- panteón, m;
  cementerio, m
gravel -- cascajo, m;
  grava, f
gray -- gris
grease -- grasa, f
great -- grande; famoso
green -- verde
greenhouse -- vernadero,
  m
greet -- saludar
grey -- gris
grocer -- abacero, m
groceries -- abarrotes,
  m
ground -- suelo, m;
  tierra, f
ground feed -- molina, f
grow -- crecer
  (g. plants) cultivar
guard -- guardar;
  guardia, f,m
guilty -- culpable
gulch -- cañada, f;
  quebrada, f
gulf -- golfo, m
gun -- fúsil, m
  (shotgun) escopeta, f
gun cabinet -- vitrina
  de armas
gun shot -- tiro, m; dis-
  paro, m; balazo, m

H

hair -- pelo, m; cabello, m
(h. cut) corte de pelo
(h. dryer) secadora de cabello, f
(h. net) redecilla, f
hairbrush -- cepillo para el cabello, m
hairy -- peludo; velludo
half -- media; mitad, f (noun)
(h.brother) media hermano
(h.sister) media hermana
hall -- salón
halt -- alto; hacer alto; parar
ham -- jamón, m
hammer -- martillo, m
hand -- mano, f
hand (verb) -- entregar
handbag -- maleta, f
handcuffs -- esposas; manilla, f
handsome -- guapo
hanger -- gancho
hang up -- colgar
happen -- suceder; pasar; ocurrir
happy -- feliz; contento; alegre

hard -- duro
hard (difficult) -- difícil
harm -- dañar; daño, m
hash -- picado, m
hat -- sombrero, m
hate -- odiar; odio, m
have -- tener (auxiliary) haber
he -- él
head -- cabeza, f
(h. ache) dolor de cabeza, f
(h. board) cabecera de una coma, f
health -- salud, f
healthy -- de buena salud
hear -- oír; oír decir
hearing -- audiencia, f
heart -- corazón, m
hearth -- hogar, m
heat -- calor, m
(to heat) calentar
heater -- calorífero, m; calentador
heavy -- pesado; grueso
hedge -- seto, m; barrera, f
heel -- tacón, m
height -- altura, f; estatura, f
Helen -- Elena
hell -- infierno, m
hello --¿que húbole?; ¡oiga! ¡hola!

127

help -- ayudar; ayuda, f;
   asistir
hem -- dobladillo, m
hen -- gallina, f
Henry -- Enrique
her -- (direct object) la
   (indirect object)le
   (preposition) ella
   (possessive) de
   ella, su
hers -- el suyo; la suya;
   los suyos; las suyas
herb -- hierba, f
here -- aquí; acá
hernia -- hernia, f
hibiscus -- hibisco, m
hide -- piel, f; cuero, m;
   esconder; ocultar
hidden -- escondido
high -- alto
high priced -- caro;
   costoso
highway -- carretera, f
hill -- sierra, f; loma, f;
   cerro, m; colina, f
him -- (direct object) le,
   lo
hip -- cadera, f
hire -- ocupar; dar
   empleo
his -- (possessive adjec-
   tive) su;
   (possessive pro-
   noun) el suyo; la
   suya; los suyos;
   las suyas

history -- historia, f
hit -- golpear; pegar
hive -- (for bees)
   colmena, f
hoe -- azadón, m; azada, f
hog -- marrano, m
hole -- (in wall) abertura,f
   (in fence) hoyo, m;
   agujero, m
   (in ground) pozo,
   m; hueco, m
holiday -- día de fiesta
home -- hogar, m; casa f
   (at home) en casa
honey -- miel
honeydew -- mielada, f
hook -- gancho, m;
   anzuelo, m
hope -- esperar;
   esperaza, f
horn -- (auto) bocina, f;
   pito, m
   (animal) cuerno, m
horse -- caballo, m
hose -- (stockings)
   medias, f
   (garden h.)
   manguera, f
hospital -- hospital,m
hot -- caliente
   (of a day, etc.)
   caluroso
   (h. house) inverna-
   culo, m

hotel -- hotel, m
hour -- hora, f
house -- casa, f; hogar,
 m; domicilio, m
household goods --
 menaje de casa, m;
 muebles, m
housekeeper -- ama de
 llaves; doméstica
housemaid -- criada, f
houseshoes -- sandalias
 pantufla
housewife -- ama de casa
how? --¿como?
however -- sin embargo
how many? --¿cuántos
 (as)?
how much? --¿cuánto (a)?
hundred -- ciento (cien)
hunger -- hambre, f
hungry -- (to be) tener
 hambre
hunt -- cazar
 (h, for) buscar
hunter -- cazador, m
hurry -- darse prisa;
 apresurarse;
 ¡andale (a)!
hurt -- (wound) herir
 (cause pain) doler
 (the feelings)
 lastimar
husband -- esposo, m;
 marido, m

hutch -- (chest) arca, f;
 cofre, m
hyacinth -- jacinto, m
hydrangea -- hortensia, f
hydrant -- llave

I

I -- yo
ice -- hielo, m
 (i. bucket) helera
 (i, cream) helado,
 m; nieve, f
icing -- (on a cake) capa
 de azúcar
idea -- idea, f
identification --
 identificación, f
identify -- identificar
idiot -- idiota, m, f
if -- si
ill -- enfermo; malo
illegitimate -- ilegítimo
 (i. child) hijo
 natural
illegal -- ilegal
illness -- enfermedad, f
immediately -- (at once)
 immediatamente
 (to follow i.) en
 seguida
immigrant -- inmigrante,
 m

129

immigrant inspector -- inspector de inmigración

immigrate -- inmigrar

immigration -- inmigración, f; migración, f

immoral -- inmoral

import -- importar

important -- importante

impossible -- imposible

imprison -- encarcelar; poner preso

improve -- mejorar

in -- en

inch -- pulgada, f

include -- incluir

independence -- independencia, f

independent -- independiente

Indian -- indio

indoors -- en casa

industry -- industria, f

in front of -- delante de

inhabitant -- habitante, m

injury -- daño, m

injured -- lisiado, m

ink -- tinta, f

innocent -- inocente

insane -- loco

insect -- insecto, m

inside -- dentro

inspect -- inspeccionar; examinar

inspector -- inspector, m

instead of -- en vez de; en lugar de

insulin -- insulina, f

intend -- pensar; tener la intención; intentar

intention -- intención, f

interest -- interés, m

interior -- interior, m

interlining -- entretela, f

interpret -- interpretar

investigate -- investigar

investigation -- investigación

invite -- invitar; convidar

iodine -- yodo, m

iris -- iris, f

iron -- hierro, m; fierro, m

(i. clothes) planchar; plancha, f

ironing board -- tabla de planchar

ironwork -- herraje, m

irrigate -- regar

irrigation -- regación, f; riego, m

island -- isla, f

it -- lo, la

Italian -- italiano (a)

Italy -- Italia

itch -- sarna, f

its -- su
ivory -- marfil, m
ivy -- hiedra, f

J

jack -- gato, m; jacke, m
jacket -- chaqueta, f
jail -- cárcel, f; bote, m
jam -- compotera
James -- Jaime
Jane -- Juana
janitor -- portero, m;
conserje, m
January -- enero, m
jar -- chirrido; jarro, m
jaw -- quijada, f;
mandibula, f
jeep -- jeepe, m
jelly -- jalea, f
jeweler -- joyero, m
jewelery -- joyas, f
Joe -- Jose; Pepe
John -- Juan
join -- juntar; unir;
un unida,f
joint -- unida, f
Josephine -- Josefina
judge -- juzgar; juez, m
jug -- jarro, m
juice -- jugo, m; toronja;
naranja
July -- julio, m
jump -- brincar; saltar

June -- junio, m
jury -- jurado, m
justice of peace -- juez
de paz

K

keep -- guardar
kennel -- (of a dog)
perrera, f
ketchup -- salsa de
tomato y setas, f
key -- llave, f
khaki -- kaki, m; caqui, m
kid (goat) -- cabrito, m
kidnap -- secuestrar
kidnaper -- secuestrador,
m
kidnaping -- secuestro, m
kidney -- riñón, m
kill -- matar
kind -- clase, f; tipo, m;
bondadoso
kitchen -- cocina, f
kitchen utensils --
batería (trastos) de
cocina
kitten -- gatito, m
(of a cat) parir
knead -- amasar

knee -- rodilla, f
knife -- navaja, f;
cuchillo, m
(large k.) machete,
m
(pen k.) cortapluma,
m

131

knot -- nudo, m
know -- saber
    (be acquainted)
    conocer
    (let know) avisar

L

labor -- labor,f; trabajo,
    m; trabajar
laborer -- trabajador, m;
    jornalero, m
lace -- (of shoes, etc.)
    cordón, m
lack -- faltar; falta, f
lacquer -- laca, f
ladder -- escalera, f
ladle -- cucharón; cazo, m
lady -- dama; señora, f
lake -- lago, m; laguna, f
lamb -- cordero, m
    (l. chops) chuletas
    de cordero
lame -- cojo
lamp -- lámpara
land -- tierra, f; terreno,
    m
landlord -- patrón, m
language -- idioma, m;
    lengua, f
lard -- manteca, f
large -- grande
    (very large)
    grandote
larger -- más grande

largest -- el or la mas
    grande
lasso -- lazo, m
last -- último; pasado
    (to last) durar
last night -- anoche
late -- tarde
later -- más tarde;
    después
lately -- últimamente;
    recientemente
latter -- este (a)
laundry -- lavendería, f
lavatory -- lavatorio;
    lavamanos
law -- ley, f
lawn -- prado, m
lawn mower -- máquina
    segadora
lawyer -- abogado, m;
    licenciado, m
laxative -- laxante, m;
    purga, f
laziness -- desidia, f;
    pereza, f
lazy -- flojo, perezoso
leaf -- hoja, f
lead -- plomo, m
lean -- flaco
learn -- aprender
least -- el or la menor
    (at least) a lo
    menos; por lo
    menos

leather -- cuero, m
leave -- salir; dejar;
    partir
leaves -- ojas
left -- izquierdo
leg -- pierna, f
legal -- legal
legally -- legalmente
lemon -- limón, m
    (l.ade) limonada
    (l. juice) jugo de
    limón
lend -- prestar
length -- largo, m;
    longitud, m
less -- menos
lesson -- lección, f
let -- dejar; permitir
letters -- letras, f
    (correspondence)
    correro, m
lettuce -- lechuga, f
level -- plano; llano;
    (instrument) nivel
level -- emparejar;
    nivelar
lever -- palanca, f
liberate -- libertar;
    librar
liberty -- libertad, f
license -- licencia, f
    (l. plates) placas, f
lid -- cobertera, f; tapa f

lie -- mentir; mentira, f
lie -- decir (echar);
    mentiras
lie down -- ascostarse;
    tendarse
life -- vida, f
lift -- levantar; alzar
light -- luz, f; luminar
light (verb) -- encender;
    prender
light -- (color) claro
    (electric l.) luz
    eléctrica
    (l. globe) foco, m
    (l. weight) ligero
lighter -- encendedor
like (verb) -- gustar
like -- (similar) seme-
    jante
    (the same) como;
    lo mismo que
limbs -- ramas
lime -- limón, lima, f
limit -- límite, m
line -- línea, f; raya, f
linen -- lino, m
    (clean l.) ropa
    limpia, f
    (dirty l.) ropa
    sucia, f
lining -- (of a garment,
    etc.) forro, m
linoleum -- linóleo, m

linseed -- (oil) aceite
de linaza, m
lint -- hilas, f
lip -- labio, m
lipstick -- lápiz para los
labios, m
liquid -- líquido, m
list -- lista, f
listen -- escuchar
little -- poco
(l. size) pequeno;
chico; chiquito
(l. quantity) poco
live -- vivir
liver -- hígado
living -- vida, f;
subsistencis, f
(l. room) sala
load -- carga, f; cargar
loaders -- cargadores, m
lobster -- langosta
local -- local
lock -- candado, m;
cerrar con llave
long -- largo
longer -- (time) mas
tiempo
look at -- mirar
look for -- buscar
loose -- suelto
loosen -- aflojar; soltar
lose -- perder
lotion -- loción, f

Louis -- Luis
Louise -- Luisa
love -- amar; querer a
low -- bajo; abajo
lower -- mas bajo;
mas abajo
lubricating oil -- aceite
lubricante, m
luck -- suerte, f
lukewarm -- tibio;
templado
lunch -- lonche, m;
merienda, f
lunch counter --
lonchería, f
lungs -- pulmones, m

M

macaroni -- macarrones,
m; fideo
machine -- máquina, f
mad -- enojado
magazine -- revista, f
mahogany -- coafa, f
maid -- criada, f
mail -- correo, m
main boss -- mero gallo
maintain -- mantener
sostener
maize -- milo maize
make -- hacer

malt -- malta, m;
(m. vinegar)
vinagre de malta, m
mamma -- mamá, f
man -- hombre, m
manager -- gerente, m;
director, m
mangos -- mangos
manner -- modo, m;
manera, f
mantle -- capa, f;
manto, m
many -- muchos (as)
map -- mapa, m
maraschino cherries --
cerezas en marras-
quino, f
marble -- mármol, m
March -- marza, m
march -- marchar
mare -- yegua, f
marigold -- caléndula;
maraville, f
mark -- marca, f; marcar
market -- mercado, m
marriage -- casamiento,
m; matrimonio
marriage certificate --
certificado de
matrimonio
maroon -- (color)
marrón, m
marry -- casarse con

Martha -- Marta
Mary -- María
mash -- puré
(m. potatoes)
puré de patatas, m
mason -- albañil, m
match -- cerilla, f
matter -- asunto, m;
negocio, m
mattress -- colchón, m
May -- mayo, m
may -- poder (to be able)
maybe -- tal vez; quizás
mayonnaise -- mayonesa, f
mayor -- alcalde, m
presidente municipal
meal -- comida, f;
harina de maíz
mean -- querer decir
meanwhile -- mientras
tanto
measles -- (German)
rubéola, f
measure -- medida, f
meat -- carne, f
meat market -- carni-
cería, f
mechanic -- mecánico, m
medicine -- medicina, f
meet -- encontrar
(become acquainted)
concer

135

meeting -- mitin, m;
  junta, f
melt -- (soften) ablandar
member -- miembro, m
mend -- (darn) zurcir
menstruation --
  menstruación
menu -- lista, f
merchant -- comerciante,
  m
meringue -- merengue, m
message -- mensaje, m;
  recado, m
metal -- metal, m
Mexican -- mexicano(a)
Mexico -- Mexico;
  Méjico
middle -- medio
midnight -- medianoche, f
midwife -- partera, f
mildew -- mildeu, m
mile -- milla, f
milk -- leche, f
mill -- molina, f
miller -- milonero, m
mince -- desmenuzar
  (m.meat) carne
  picado, f
mine -- (possessive pro-
  noun) el mío; la mía;
  los míos; las mías
mine -- mina, f
miner -- minero, m

mineral -- mineral, m
mink -- visón, m
minor -- menor (de edad)
mint -- (candy) menta, f
minus -- menos
minute -- minuto, m
mirror -- espejo, m
Miss -- señorita, f; Srta.
mistake -- falta, f;
  error, m
mix -- mezclar;
  (m. salad) aderezar
mixer -- (electric)
  mezclador eléctrico, m
molasses -- melaza, f
mole -- lunar, m
moment -- momento, m
Monday -- lunes, m
money -- dinero, m
month -- mes, m
moon -- luna, f
mop -- (implement)
  mop, m
more -- mas
morning -- mañana. f
mosquito -- zancudo
moth -- polilla, f
mothball -- bola de
  naftalina, f
mother -- madre, f
mother-in-law --
  suegra, f
motor -- motor, m

mount -- montar;
montura
mountain -- montana, f
mouse trap -- ratonera, f
mouth -- boca, f
move -- mover
movie -- cina, m
mow -- cortar
mower -- máquina para
cortar pastura
Mr. -- señor, Sr.
Mrs. -- señora, Sra.
much -- mucho
mud -- lodo
mulberry -- (fruit) mora,
f
mule -- mula, f
murder -- asesinar
murderer -- asesinato, m
mushrooms -- setas
music -- música, f
musician -- músico, m
mustache -- bigote, m
mustard -- mostaza, f
my -- mi

N

nail -- clavo, m
name -- nombre, m
name -- (to be) llamarse
nap -- (sleep) siesta, f
napkin, large --
servilleta, f

napkin, small -- toallita
narcissus -- narciso, m
narrow -- angosto;
estrecho
nation -- nación, f
nationality --
nacionalidad, f
native -- native (a)
naturalize -- naturalizar
naturalization --
naturalización, f
nausea -- náusea, f
necessary -- necesario
neck -- cuello, m;
pescuezo, m
need -- necesitar; faltar
needle -- aguja, f
neighbor -- vecino (a)
neither -- ni; tampoco
neither -- (nor) ni . . . ni
nephew -- sobrino, m
nest -- (bird's) nido, m
net wire -- alambre
de tela
never -- nunca; jamás
nevertheless -- sin
embargo
new -- nuevo
newspaper -- periódico,
m; diario, m
next -- próximo; que
viene; siguiente
nickname -- apodo, m

137

niece -- sobrina, f
night -- noche, f
nightfall -- anochecer, m
nightgown -- camizón
nine -- nueve
nineteen -- diez y nueve
ninety -- noventa
ninth -- noveno
nippers -- alicates, m
nipple -- pezón, m
no -- n0
nobody -- nadie
noise -- ruido, m
none -- ninguna (o)
noon -- mediodía, m
nor -- ni
north -- norte, m
North America --
    norteamericano (a)
nose -- nariz, f
not -- no
nothing -- nada
November -- noviembre,
    m
now -- ahora
    (right n.) ahorita
nowadays -- hoy día
nozzle -- (of a hose or
    pipe) boquilla, f
nurse -- nodriza, f;
    enfermera, f
        (children's n.)
        niñera, f

nut -- nuez, f
nutmeg -- nuez moscada;
    nuez de especia, f

nylon -- nilón, nylon, m
    (stockings) medias
    . de nilón, f

O

oak -- roble, m; encino, m
oath -- juramento, m
oath -- (to take o.) prestar
    juramento; tomar jura-
    mento; declarar bajo
    juramento
oatmeal -- harina de
    avena, f
oats -- avena, f
observe -- observar
obtain -- obtener
ocean -- océano, m
occupation -- oficio, m;
    ocupación, f
occupied -- ocupado
occupy -- ocupar
occur -- ocurrir;
    suceder
October -- octubre, m
odor -- olor m
        (fragrance)
        perfume; aroma, m
of -- de
offense -- ofensa, f
offer -- oferta, f

138

office -- oficina, f
officer -- oficial, m;
   dignatario, m
official -- oficial, m
often -- a menudo
oil -- aceite, m
oilcloth -- hule;
   linóleo, m
okra -- bombones
old -- viejo
older -- mayor
oleander -- adelfa, f;
   baladre, m
olive -- (tree) olivo, m
   (fruit) aceituna;
   oliva, f
on -- en; sobre; encima
   de
once -- una vez
   (at once) en seguida
one -- uno; una
one-eyed -- tuerto (a)
onion -- cebolla, f
only -- único; solo;
   solamente
opal -- ópalo, m
open -- abrir
opened -- abierto
opportunity --
   oportunidad, f
or -- o
orange -- (fruit) naranja, f
   (tree) naranjo, m

orangeade -- naranjada, f
orchard -- huerto
orchid -- orquídea, f
order -- mandar
orphan -- huérfano, m
ostrich -- avestruz, m
other -- otro
ought -- deber
our -- nuestro
ours -- el nuestro, etc.
out -- fuera; afuera
oven -- horno, m
over -- sobre; encima de
overalls -- overoles, m
overcoat -- abrigo, m;
   sobretodo, m
overshoe -- chanclo, m
   (for snow) galocha, f
over yonder -- allá
owe -- deber
owner -- dueño, m
oxygen -- oxigeno, m
oyster -- ostra, f

P

pack -- llevar
package -- bulto, m;
   paquete, m
packing shed -- bodega, f
page -- página, f
pain -- dolor, m; doler
paint -- (to paint) pintar
   (painting on wall)
   pintura, f

139

painter -- pintor, m
pair -- par, m
pajamas -- pijamas
pan -- cazuela, f
panties -- calzones
pantry -- despensa, f
pants -- pantalones, m
panty hose -- panti media
panzy -- pensamiento
papa -- papá, m
papaya -- papaya
paper -- papel, m
   (p. towels) toalla
   de papel
paraffin -- parafina, f
paralysis -- parálisis, f
pardon -- perdonar;
   perdon, m
parents -- padres, m
park -- parque, m;
   estacionarse
parsley -- perejil, m
parsnip -- chirivía, f
part -- parte, f; partir
party -- partido, m;
   grupo, m
   (of pleasure, etc.)
   partida, f
pass -- pasar; paso, m
passage -- pasaje, m
passenger -- pasajero, m
passport -- pasaporte, m
past -- pasado; ultimo

paste -- pasta, f
   (glue) engomar;
   engrudar
pastry -- (dough) pasta, f
pasture -- pastura, f;
   pasto, m
patch -- (mend)
   remiendo, m
path -- sendero, m;
   vereda, f
pattern -- modelo, m
   (dressmaking)
   patrón, m
Paul -- Pablo
paved -- pavimentado
pavement -- pavimento, m
   (sidewalk) acera, f
pavilion -- pabellón, m
paw -- pata, f
pay -- pagar
pay day -- día de pagos
pea -- chícharo, m
   (dry or split p)
   chícharo secos, m
   (sweet p. - flower)
   chícharo de olor, m
peach -- (fruit) melocotón,
   m; durazno, m
   (p. tree)
   melocotonero, m
   (p. color) color de
   melocotón, m
peacock -- pavo real;
   pavón, m

peanut --cacahuate, m
(p. butter) mante-
quilla de cacahuate
pear -- pera, f
pearl -- perla, f
peasant -- paisano
pecan -- nueces
peel -- piel, f
pen -- (writing) pluma, f
pen -- (for stock) corral,
m
pencil -- lápiz, m
penicillin -- penicilina, f
penny -- centavo, m
people -- gente, f;
pueblo, m
pepper -- (black)
pimiento, m
(bell p.) chile
dulce
(green p.) chile
verde, m
(p. mint) menta, f
(p. shaker)
pimentero
percolator -- (coffee)
colador de café, m
perfume -- perfume
perhaps -- tal vez;
quizás; puede ser
perjury -- perjurio, m
permanently --
permanentemente
permission -- permiso, m;
permissión, f

permit -- permitir;
permiso, m
person -- persona, f
petticoat -- faldas, f
pewter -- peltre, m
pheasant -- faisán, m
phlox -- flox, m
photo -- foto
photograph -- fotografía;
retrato, m
piano -- piano
pick -- pico, m
pick -- (choose) escoger
pick up -- levantar; coger
pickle -- pepino
picture -- (person)
retrato, m
(on wall) cuadro, m
(painting) pintura, f
picture film -- película, f
picture show -- cine, m
pie -- pastel, m
(p. crust) pasta, f
piece -- pedazo, m;
pieza, f
pill -- píldora, f
pillar -- pilar, m;
columna, f
pillow -- almohada, f
(p. case) funda, f
pimp -- palo blanco, m;
alcahuete, m
pimple -- granujo, m;
espinilla, f

141

pin -- alfiler, m;
broche, m
pinafore -- delantal de
niño, m
pincers -- pinzas, f
pine -- (tree) pino, m
pineapple -- piña
pink -- color de rosa, m
pint -- (measure) pinta, f
pinto bean -- frijol pinto
pipe -- tubo, m; pipa, f
pistol -- pistola, f
pitcher -- jarra
pits -- (small box)
viruelas, f
pitted -- pitada
place -- lugar, m;
sitio, m
plant -- plantar; planta,
f; sembrar
plate -- plato, m;
platillo, m
platform -- plataforma, f
platinum -- platino, m
platter -- fuente, f;
plato, m; trinchero, m
play -- jugar; juego, m
plaza -- plaza, f
please -- gustar; agradar
please -- por favor
pleat -- plieuge, m
pleurisy -- pleuresía, f
pliers -- pinzas, f

plow -- arar; arado, m;
cultivar
plumber -- plomero, m
plums -- ciruelas
pneumonia -- pulmonía, f
poach --˙(eggs) escalfar
pocket -- bolsillo, m
pocket book -- bolso, m;
portamonedas, f
point -- punto, m; punta, f
poison -- veneno, m;
envenenar
pole -- palo, m
police force -- la policía
police officer --
el policía
polish -- (metal) pulir;
(furniture & shoes)
dar brillo
poor -- pobre
(lean) flaco
popcorn -- palomitas
poplar -- álamo, m
poppy -- amapola;
adormidera, f
porch -- (of house)
portal, m
porcupine -- puerco
espín, m
pore -- poro, m
pork -- carne de cerdo, f
(salt p.) tocino, m
(p chops) chuletas
de puerco

port -- puerto, m
porter -- cargador, m;
   portero, m
portrait -- retrato, m
possible -- posible
post -- poste, m;
   palo, m
postmaster --
   administrador (jefe)
   de correos, m
post office -- correo, m;
   estafeta, f
pot -- olla, f
   (f. pot) tiesto, m
potato -- (Irish) papa, f;
   patata, f; fritos;
   asadas
pot roast -- carne de
   horno
pottery -- loza
pound -- libra, f
pour -- (coffee, milk,
   etc.) servir
pouring -- (of rain)
   torrencial
powder -- polvo, m
power -- poder, m;
   fuerza, f
pox -- (small p.)
   viruelas, f
   (chicken p.)
   viruelas falsas, f
pray -- rezar

prayer -- rezo, m
   (p. meeting)
   reunión para
   rezar, f
preceding -- anterior
prefer -- preferir
pregnant -- preñada
prepare -- preparar
prescription --
   prescripción
present -- presente
   (gift) regalo
present -- presentar
preserves -- conservas
president -- presidente, m
pressing -- (garment)
   planchado, m
pressure -- presión, f
   (of hand) apretón, m
   (weight) peso, m
pretty -- bonito; lindo
price -- precio, m
priest -- cura, m;
   sacerdote, m
prison -- prisión, m;
   cárcel, f; juzgado, m
proceedings -- actas, f;
   autos, m;
   procedimientos, m
prohibit -- prohibir
promise -- prometer;
   promesa, f
promoter -- promotor, m;
   empresario, m;
   constancia, f

proper -- correcto
property -- propiedad, f
protect -- proteger
protein -- proteína, f
prune -- (fruit) ciruela
pasa
(to cut) cortar;
reducir
pruning knife -- podadera,
f
prove -- probar;
comprobar, m
pudding -- flan
pull -- estirar; tirar;
arrancar
pullet -- polla, f
pulp -- (of fruit) carne, f
pulse -- (to take person's
p.) tomar el pulso (a)
pump -- bomba, f
(for water, etc.)
aguatocha, f
pumpkin -- calabaza, f
(plant) calabacera
punch -- (drink) ponche, m
(p. bowl) ponchera, f
punish -- castigar
pupil -- alumno (a);
estudiante, m or f;
discípulo (a)
purchase -- comprar;
compra, f
pure -- puro

purple -- púrpura, f
purpose -- objecto, m
purse -- bolsa, f;
portamonedas, m
push -- empujar
put -- poner; colocar
put on -- ponerse
puzzle -- (game) dejar
perplejo

Q

quail -- codorniz, m
quarrel -- barulla, f;
disgusto, m
quart -- cuarto, m
quarter -- cuarto, m
queen -- reina, f
question -- pregunta;
cuestión, f
quick -- pronto
quickly -- pronto
quilt -- colcha, f; cobija
quince -- (fruit & trees)
membrillo, m
(q. jelly) jalea de
membrillo, f
quinine -- quinina, f
quit -- abandonar; dejar

R

rabbit -- conejo, m;
liebre, f
rabies -- rabia;
hidrofobia, f

144

rack -- percha, f
raccoon -- tejón, m
radiator -- (for car)
  radiator, m
radio -- radio, f
radish -- rábano, m
rag -- trapo, m
railroad -- ferrocarril, m
  (r. track) rieles, m;
  traque, m
rain -- llover; lluvia, f
raise -- criar
raisin -- pasa, f
rake -- rastra, f; rastrear;
  rastrillo, m
Ralph -- Rafael; Raul
ranch -- rancho, m
rancher -- ranchero, m
ranch foreman --
  caporal, m
rape -- rapto, m;
  estupro, m
rasp -- raspador, m
rat -- rata, f
rattlesnake -- víbora, f;
  cascabel, m
ravel -- deshilar
ravine -- arroyo, m;
  canada, f
raw -- crudo
razor -- razura, f
  (r. blades) hojas
read -- leer
ready -- listo

reap -- cosechar
reason -- razón, f; causa,
  f
receipt -- recibo, m
receive -- recibir
recently -- recientemente
recipe -- receta, f
record -- record, m;
  constancia, f; registrar;
  apuntar
rectum -- recto, m
red -- rojo, m
reenlisted --
  reenganchado
refrigerator --
  refrigerador, m;
  enfriadera, f
rein -- rienda, f
relative -- pariente, m
relax -- aflojar; soltar
release -- libertar;
  poner en libertad
remain -- permanecer;
  durar; quedarse; estarse
remember -- recordar;
  acodarse
renew -- renovar
rent -- rentar; arrendar;
  alquilar
rent -- renta, f
repaint -- pintar de
  nuevo
repair -- reparar;
  componer

repair -- reparto, m
report -- informe, m;
  reporte, m; reportar;
  informar
republic -- república, f
requirement -- requisito,
  m
reseal -- resellar
reside -- residir;
  morar; vivir
residence -- residencia,
  f: domicilio, m; casa, f;
  morada, f
resources -- los bienes;
  riquezas, f
rest -- descansar;
  reposar
resume -- reasumir
retail -- al por menor
return -- regresar;
  volver; regreso, m;
  vuelta, f
reveal -- revelar;
  monstrar; demonstrar
revolver -- revolver, m
rib -- costilla, f
rice -- arroz, m
rich -- rico
Richard -- Ricardo
ride -- (auto) viajar en
  auto
  (train) viajar en
  tren
  (horse) montar a
  caballo

rifle -- rifle, m
right -- derecho, m;
  razón, f
  (direction) derecha
rights -- derechos
rind -- (of bacon) piel, f
  (of cheese) costra, f
  (of fruit) cáscara,
  corteza, f
ring -- anillo, m;
  sortija, f
rinse -- (of clothes)
  enjuagar
ripe -- maduro; sazonado
river -- río, m
road -- camino, m
roast -- asar
roast beef -- bif asada;
  rosbif, m
roasting ears -- helotes,
  m
rob -- robar
robber -- ladrón, m
robbery -- robo, m
robe -- robe
  (bath r.) albornoz, m
Robert -- Roberto
rock -- piedra, m
rocker -- (chair)
  mecedora, f
rod -- varilla, f
roll -- rollo, m
  (of bread)
  panecillo, m

roof -- techo, m
room -- cuarto, m;
  pieza, f
rooster -- gallo, m
roots -- raíces
rope -- reata, f; lazo, m;
  mecate, m; soga, f;
  cuerda, f
rose -- rosa, f
  (r. bud) capullo de
    rosa, m
  (r. bush) rosal, m
rosé -- (of wine) rosado
rouge -- colorete, m
rough -- áspero
round -- redondo
route -- rumbo, m; ruta, f
row -- surco, m
rug -- alfombra, f
rule -- regla, f
rum -- ron, m
run -- correr
rush -- tener prisa

        S

saccharin -- sacarina, f
sack -- saco, m;
  costal, m
sad -- triste
safe -- salvo; seguro
sage -- salvia
sailor -- marinero, m
salad -- ensalada, f
  (s. bowl) macedonia, f

  (s. dressing)
    mayonesa, f
  (fruit s.) macedonia
    de frutas, f
salary -- sueldo, m;
  salario, m
salmon -- salmón, m
saloon -- cantina, f;
  salón, m
salt -- sal, f
  (s. shaker) salero
same -- mismo; igual
sand -- arena, f
sandal -- sandalia, f
sandpaper -- lija, f
sandwich -- sandwich, m;
  emparedado, m
sardines -- sardina, m
satisfied -- contento;
  satisfecho; conforme
Saturday -- sábado, m
sauce -- salsa, f
saucer -- platillo, m
sauerkraut --
  choucroute, f
sausage -- chorizo, m;
  salchicha, f
save -- salvar
  (keep) guardar;
    conservar;
    reservar
saw -- serrucho, m
say -- decir

scab -- (of wound)
   costra, f
scales -- balanzas, f;
   romana, f
scar -- cicatriz, f;
   sena, f
scar -- (cut) cortada, f
scarf -- chalina
school -- escuela, f
scissors -- tijeras, f
scorpion -- alacrán;
   escorpión, m
scrambled eggs --
   huevos revueltos
screen -- (window s.) tela
screw -- tornillo
   (s. driver) almador,
   m; desarmador, m
scrub -- fregar
scythe -- alfanje, m; hoz,
   f
seal -- (s. jar) cerrar
seamstress --
   costurera, f
search -- registrar
search for -- buscar
season -- estación, f
seat -- asiento, m
seated -- sentado
second -- segundo, m
secretary -- secretario,
   m
sedative -- sedativo, m

see -- ver
seed -- semilla, f
   (s. bed) almárcigo,
   m
seek -- buscar
seem -- parecer
sell -- vender
send -- mandar; enviar;
   expedir
sentence -- condenar;
   sentenciar; condena, f;
   fallo, m; sentencia, f
sentence -- frase, f
September --
   septiembre, m
servant -- criado (a);
   mozo (a); doméstico (a)
serve -- servir
set -- (to place) colocar
   (s. table) poner
   (s. clock) regular
   el peloj
   (s. out plants)
   plantar
seven -- siete
seventeen -- diez y siete
seventy -- séptimo
several -- varios (as);
   algunos (as)
sew -- coser
sewing -- costura, f
   (s. machine)
   maquina de coser,
   f

sex -- sexo, m
shallot -- chalote, m
shampoo -- champú
sharp -- (of edges)
    afilado; cortante
sharpen -- (knives) afilar;
    amolar
shave -- afeitar (se);
    rasurar
shawl -- chal, m
she -- ella
shears -- tijeras
shed -- casa de
    implementos
sheet -- sábana, f
shelf -- estante; anaquel,
    m
shell -- (peas, etc.)
    cascara
        (to shell) desvainar
sherbet -- sorbete, m
sheriff -- sherife, m;
    jerife, m
sherry -- jerez, m
        (dry s.) jerez seco,
        m
shin -- espinilla, f
shine -- brillar
ship -- buque, m; vapor,
    m; barco, m
shirt -- camisa, f
shoe -- zapato, m
shoe store -- zapatería, f

shoot -- tirar; disparar;
    fusilar
shop -- tienda, f; taller, m
shore -- orilla, f
short -- corto, bajo
        (s. man) capo, m
shot -- bala, m; balazo,
    m; disparo, m
shoulder -- hombro, m
shovel -- pala, f
show -- enseñar; mostrar
shrimp -- camarones
shrub -- arbusto, m;
    matajo, m
shrubbery -- arbustos
shut -- cerrar
shutter -- (window)
    contraventana, f;
    postigo, m
        (of camera)
        obturador, m
Siamese -- (S. cat) gato
    siamés, m
sick -- enfermo; malo
side -- lado, m
sidewalk -- acera, f;
    banqueta, f
sieve -- (utensil)
    cedazo, m
sift -- cribar
sight -- vista, f
sign -- firmar; signo, m;
    señal, f; seña, f

149

signature -- firma, f
silk -- seda, f
sill -- (of door) umbral, m
(of window)
alféizar; ante-
pecho, m
silver -- plata, f
simmer -- (cooking)
hervir a fuego lento
since -- desde; pues
sing -- cantar
singe -- (a fowl)
aperdigar
single -- solo
(s. person) soltero
(a)
sink -- (kitchen s.)
fregadero
sinus -- seno, m
sir -- señor
sister -- hermana, f
sister-in-law -- cuñada, f
sit down -- sentarse
six -- seis
sixteen -- diez y seis
sixth -- sexto
sixty -- sesenta
size -- tamaño, m
skewer -- broqueta, f
skim -- (milk)
desnatar
skin -- piel, f; cutis, f
(s. of fruit) pellejo,
m; piel, f

skinny -- flaco
skirt -- falda, f
skunk -- zorillo, m
sky -- cielo, m
slacks -- pantalones
sledge hammer -- maso, f
sleep -- dormir; sueño, m
sleet -- agua nieve, f;
grajea, f
sleeve -- manga, f
sleeveless -- sin manga
slice -- lanja; tajada, f
(of fruit) raja, f
(of bread, etc.)
rebanada, f
slim -- delgado; flaco
slip -- (petticoat) fondo, m
slipper -- zapatilla, f
slow -- despacio; lento
slowly -- despacio;
lentamente
small -- pequeño; chico
smallpox -- viruelas, f
smoke -- fumar; humo, m
smooth -- suave; liso;
llano
smuggle -- pasar dé
contrabando
smuggler -- contrabandista
m
snack -- piscolabis
snail -- caracol, m

snake -- víbora, f; culebra, f
  (rattle s.) víbora de cascabel
snap -- (clasp) cierre, m
  (s. fastener) botón de presión, m
snapdragon -- (flower) dragón
sneeze -- estornudar
snow -- nevar; nieve, f
so -- así; tan
so many -- tantos (as)
so much -- tanto (a)
soap -- jabón, m
  (s. dish) jabonera, f
  (s. suds) jabonaduras, f
sock -- calcetín, m
soda -- sosa
soda-pop -- soda
sofa -- sofá, f
soft -- suave; blando
  (s. boiled eggs) pasado por agua
soil -- tierra, f; suelo, m
soldier -- soldado, m
sole -- (of shoe) suela, f
solicit -- solicitar
some -- alguno
somebody -- alguien; alguna persona

something -- algo; alguna cosa
son -- hijo, m
son-in-law -- yerno, m
soon -- pronto
soot -- hollín, m
sort -- clase, f; modo, m
soup -- caldo, m
sour -- ácido, agrio
  (s. milk) agrio
south -- sur, m; sud
sow -- sembrar
space -- espacio, m
spaghetti -- fideo, m
Spain -- Espana
Spaniard -- español (a)
Spanish -- español, m;
  (adj.) español (a)
spark plug -- bujía, f
speak -- hablar
special -- especial
spectacles -- anteojos, m; lentes, m
speed -- velocidad, f
spend -- (money) gastar (time) pasar
spice -- especia, f; sabor, m
  (s. cupboard) especiero, m
spider -- araña, f
  (s. web) telaraña, f
spill -- derramar

spinach -- acelga, f;
espinaca, f
spine -- espinazo, m;
columna vertebral, f
sponge -- esponja, f
(s. cake) bizcocho,
m
spool -- (for thread)
bobina, carreta
spoon -- cuchara, f
(iced tea) cuchara
de té
(tea) cucharita
(soup) cuchara de
caldo
(serving) cuchara
de servir
spoonful -- cucharada, f
sports -- deportes
spot -- mancha, f
(the place) sitio,
m; lugar, m
spotted -- manchado
sprain -- torcer
spray -- (poison)
envenenar
sprayer -- regadora, f
(plants s.) regadora,
f; máquina
envenedora
spring -- primavera, f
sprinkler -- regadera
spurs -- espuelas, f

square -- cuadrado, m
(s. in town) plaza, f
squash -- calabaza, f
squirrel -- ardilla, f
stain -- manchar
(s. remover)
quitamanchas, m
stainless steel -- acero
inoxidable, m
stairs -- escaleras, f
stalk -- (plant) tallo, m
stamp -- estampar
(for letters) sello, m
(rubber s.)
estampilla, f
staples -- grampas, f
star -- estrella, f
starch -- almidón
(spray s.) espray
de almidón
start -- empezar;
comenzar; principiar
state -- estado, m;
declarar
statement --
declaración, f
station -- estación, f
stationery -- papelería, f
stay -- quedarse;
permanecer
steak -- (beef) biftec, m
steal -- robar
steam -- vapor, m

stem -- (of tree) tronco, m
(of plant) tallo, m
(of glass) pie, m
step -- paso, m
step-daughter -- hijastra,
f; entenada, f
step-father -- padrastro,
m
step-mother -- madrastra,
f
step-son -- hijastro, m;
entenado, m
steps -- (stairs)
escaleras, f
sterilize -- esterilizar
stew -- cocer
stick -- palo, m; bastón, m
still -- todaviá; tranquilo
sting -- picar
stir -- agitar; revolver
stockings -- medias, f
stole -- (fur) estola, f
stomach -- estómago, m
stone -- piedra, f
stool -- tabureta, m
stop -- alto
stop up -- parar; tapar
stopper -- tapón, m;
obturador, m
story -- cuento, m;
historia, f
stove -- estufa, m
stowaway -- polizón, m

straight -- derecho;
recto; directo
strain -- (food) estirar
strainer -- filtro, m
strained -- tenso
(of muscles, etc.)
torcido
stranger -- extranjero, m
straw -- paja, f
strawberry -- fresa, f
street -- calle, f
strength -- vigor, m;
fuerza, f
stretch -- (pull) estirar
(make bigger)
enganchar
stretcher -- gancho
strike -- pegar; golpear;
golpe, f
string -- cordón, m;
cuerda, f
striped -- rayado; listado
strong -- fuerte
student -- alumno (a);
estudiante
study -- estudiar; estudio,
m
suburb -- barrio, m;
colonia, f
suddenly -- de repente
sue -- poner, una queja;
poner pleito
suffer -- sufrir; padecer

sugar -- azúcar, m
  (s. bowl) azucarero
suit -- traje, m; vestido,
  m
suit (law) -- pleito; queja,
  f
suitcase -- maleta, f;
  veliz, m
sum -- suma, f
summer -- verano, m
sun -- sol, m
sundown -- puesta del
  sol, f
sunflower -- mirasol, m
Sunday -- domingo, m
supper -- cena, f
sure -- seguro; cierto
surname -- apellido, m
surprise -- sorpresa, f;
  asombro, m
swallow -- (in throat)
  engullir
swan -- cisne, m
swear -- jurar; hacer;
  juramento
sweater -- sweter
sweet -- dulce
  (s. potato) batada f
sweetbread -- lechecillas,
  f
swim -- nadar; flotar
swimming -- natación, f
sycamore -- sicomoro, m
  falso plátano m

sympathy -- simpatía, f;
  compasíon, f
syringe -- jeringa, f
syrup -- jarabe, m
  (preserving s.)
  almíbar, m

T

table -- mesa, f
tablespoon -- cuchara, f
tablet -- tabla, f
tacos -- tacos
tack -- (nail) tachuella;
  puntilla, f
taffeta -- táfetan, m
tail -- cola, f; rabo, m
tailor -- sastre, m
tailor shop -- sastrería, f
take -- tomar; llevar;
  aceptar
take away -- quitar
take off -- quitarse
take out -- sacar
take steps to -- hacer
  arreglos
talcum powder -- talco;
  polvo de talco, m
talk -- hablar
tall -- alto
tank -- tanque, m
tangerine -- naranja
  japonese
tap -- tapón, m

154

tape -- (adhesive t.) cinta
adhesive
(t. measure) cinta
métrica, f
tapestry -- tapiz, m
tarpaulin -- lona, f:
tarpa, f
tartar sauce -- salsa de
tártaro
(cream of t.) cremor
tártaro, m
taste -- gusto, m
tattoo -- tabú m; tatuaje,
m; grabado; pintura, f
taxi -- taxi, m; carro de
sitio, m
tea -- té, m
teach -- enseñar
teacher -- maestro, m;
profesor, m
teaspoon -- cucharita, f
teeth -- dientes, m
telegram -- telegrama, f
telephone -- teléfono, m;
telefonear
television -- televisión,
TV
tell -- decir
ten -- diez
tend -- cuidar
tenth -- décimo
tepid -- tibio
tequila -- tequila, m

test -- (proof) prueba, f;
examen, m
testimony -- testimonio,
m; declaración, f
thank -- dar gracias
thanks -- gracias, f
Thanksgiving -- acción
de gracias, f
that -- (relative) que
(demonstrative)
aquel, ese
the -- el, m; la, f; los,
m; las, f
theater -- teatro, m
their -- su; sus
theirs -- el suyo, etc.
them -- (direct object)
los; las
them -- (prepositional
pronoun) ellos; ellas
then -- entonces; luego;
depues
there -- alá; allí; ahí
thermometer --
termómetro, m
these -- estos (as)
they -- ellos; ellas
thick -- grueso; denso;
espeso
thief -- ladrón, m
thin -- delgado; fino;
flaco
thing -- cosa, f

155

think -- pensar; creer
third -- tercero
thirsty -- tener sed
thirteen -- trece
thirty -- treinta
this -- este, m; esta, f
Thomas -- Tomás
thorn -- espina, f
thread -- hilo, m
three -- tres
throat -- garganta, f;
  orificio, m
through -- por
throw -- tirar; echar;
  lanzar
thumb -- pulgar, m
thunder -- trueno, m
Thursday -- jueves, m
thus -- así; de este modo
tick -- garrapata
ticket -- boleto, m;
  billete, m; tíquete, m
tie -- corbata, f
tiger -- tigre, m
tile -- tejas, f
  (for flooring)
    baldosa; losa, f
  (tile floor)
    enlosado;
    embaldosado, m
time -- (period) tiempo, m
  (numerical) vez, f
  (of day) hora, f

tin -- estaño, m; lata, f;
  hojalata, f
tire -- llanta, f;
  neumático, m
tire -- cansar
tired -- cansado
tissue paper -- papel
  de seda
to -- a; hasta
toad -- sapo, m
toadstool -- hongo, m
toast -- pan tostada, f
toaster -- tostador, m
tobacco -- tobaco, m
today -- hoy
toe -- dedo (del pie), m
toffee -- caramelo, m
together -- juntos;
  junto con
toilet -- excusado, m;
  retrete, m
  (t. paper) papel
  higiénico
tomato -- tomate, m
tomato sauce -- salsa de
  tomate, f
tomorrow -- mañana, f
tongue -- lengua, f
tongs -- tenaza, f
tonic -- tónico m
tonight -- esta noche, f
tonsil -- amigdala, f
tonsillitis -- amigalitis, f

too -- también; además
too much -- demasiado,
(adj.), demasiado
tools -- herramientas, f
tooth -- diente, m; muela, f
(t. brush) cepillo
para los dientes
(t. pick) palillo
(t.ache) dolor de
muelar, m
top -- cima, f; cumbre, f
tornado -- tornado, m
touch -- tocar
tourist -- turista, m
towel -- toalla, f
town -- pueblo, m;
población, f
toy -- jugete, m
track -- huella, f; seguir
la pista
track -- (railroad) traque,
m; rieles
tractor -- tractor, m
trail -- sendero m;
vereda, f
train -- tren, m
trap -- potrero, m;
trampa, f
trash -- basura
travel -- viajar; caminar
traveler -- viajero (a)
tray -- bandeja, f;
platillo, m

treat -- (pleasure) gusto;
placer, m
tree -- árbol, m
trial -- juzgado, m;
prueba, f
trip -- viaje, m;
excursión, f
trousers -- pantalones, m
trot -- trote, m
trowel -- (mason's)
pleta, f; palustre, m
truck -- camión, m;
troca, m; troque, m
trucker -- troquero, m
true -- verdad, f;
verdadero; sincero
trunk -- baúl, f; petaca, f
(tree t.) tronco, m
truth -- verdad,f
try -- tratar de; procurar
(trial) juzgar
tub -- baño, m
(bath t.) bañera, f;
baño, m
tube -- tubo, m
tuck -- (sew) alforza, f;
pliegue, m
Tuesday -- martes, m
tulip -- tulipán, m
turkey -- guajolote, m;
pavo, m; cócono, m
turn -- doblar; dar
vuelto (a) volver

turnip -- nabo, m
turpentine -- aguarrás, m;
  trementina, f
turquoise -- turquesa, f
turtle -- tortuga, f
  (t. soup) sopa de
    tortuga, f
twelve -- doce
twenty -- veinte
twice -- dos veces
twin -- cuate, m; gemelo,
  m
two -- dos
typewriter -- máquina
  de escribir
typhoid -- tifoidea; fiebre
  tifoidea, f

U

ugly -- feo
ulcer -- úlcera, f
umbrella -- paraguas, m
uncle -- tío, m
under -- bajo; abajo;
  debajo
underarm -- sobaco, m
undershirt -- camiseta
underwear -- calzones
uneven -- desigual
uniform -- uniforme
The United States -- Los
  Estados Unidos
unload -- descargar
unlock -- abrir

unplug -- desenchufar
untie -- (knots) deshacer
until -- hasta; hasta que
up -- arriba
  (get u.) levantarse
upon -- sobre en
upon oath -- bajo
  juramento
upset -- volcar
upstairs -- arriba
urgent -- urgente;
  importante; apremiante;
  perentorio
urinal -- orinal;
  urinario, m
urine -- orín, m
urn -- urna, f
  (for coffee) cafetera,
    f
  (for tea) telera, f
us -- (prep.) nosotros (as)
  (obj.) nos
use -- usar

V

vaccinate -- vacunar
vaccination -- vacuña, f
vacuum -- vacío, m
  (v. cleaner)
    aspirador de polvo
valid -- válido
valley -- valle, m
value -- valor, m;
  precio, m

vanilla -- vainilla, f
various -- varios (a);
    diferentes
varnish -- barniz, m
vase -- vaso, m
vaseline -- vaselina, f
veal -- ternera, f
    (v. cutlets) chuleta
    de ternera, f
vegetables -- vegetal;
    legumbres, f; verduras,
    f
veil -- velo, m
velvet -- terciopelo, m
venetian blinds --
    persianas, celosías
venison -- venado, m
vest -- chaleco, m
view -- vista, f
vine -- parral
vinegar -- vinagre, m
violate -- violar;
    infringir
visa -- visa, f;
    visar (verb)
visit -- visitar; visita, f
visitor -- visita, m or f;
    visitador, m; visitante,
    m
vitamin -- vitamina, f
vodka -- vodca, m
voice -- voz, f
voluntary -- voluntario

voluntarily --
    voluntariamente
vote -- votar; voto, m

W

wade -- vadear; andar a
    pie por el agua
wages -- sueldo, m
wagon -- vágon, m;
    carreta, f
waist -- cintura, f
wait -- esperar;
    aguardar
waiter -- mozo (a);
    criado (a); mesero (a);
    camarero (a)
walk -- andar
walking cane -- bastón
wall -- pared, f;
    muralla, f
wallet -- cartera, f
walnut -- nuez de nogal, f
want -- necesitar; querer;
    desear
war -- guerra, f
warm -- caliente; calentar
    (lukewarm) libio
    (hot) caluroso
warn -- avisar
warrant -- (of arrest)
    fallo de arresto; orden
    de arresto
wart -- verruga, f
wash -- lavar (se)

159

washerwoman --
lavandera, f
washing machine --
máquina de lavar, f
wasp -- avispa, f
(w. nest) avispero, m
watch -- reloj, m
(wrist w.) reloj de
pulsera, m
watch -- guardar; cuidar
watchmaker -- relojero, m
water -- el agua, f; regar
waterbottle --
cantimplora, f
watercress -- berros, m
watermelon -- sandía, f
wax -- cera, f
waxed paper -- papel
encerado
we -- nosotros (as)
weak -- débil
weapon -- arma, f
wear -- llevar; tener
puesto
weather -- tiempo, m
Wednesday -- miércoles,
m
weed -- yerba, f
week -- semana, f; ocho
días
week-end -- fin de
semana, m
weep -- llorar

weevil -- gorgojo, m
weigh -- pesar;
considerar
weight -- peso, m
well -- pozo, m; noria, f;
pues; bien
west -- oeste, m;
poniente, m
wet -- mojar, mojado;
húmedo
what? --¿que?
whatever -- cualquier (a)
wheat -- trigo, m
wheel -- rueda, f
wheel barrow --
carretilla, f
when? --¿cuándo?
when -- cuándo
where -- dónde
where? --¿dónde?
whether -- si
whetrock -- piedra de
afilar; amoladera, f
which? -- cuál?
which -- (relative) que
whiskey -- whiskey
white -- blanco
who? --¿quién?
who -- (relative) que;
quien
whole -- entero; todo
wholesale -- al por
mayor, en grande

whom -- a quién
whore -- ramera; puta;
  prostituta
whose -- cypo
whose? --¿de quién?
why? --¿por que?
wicker -- mimbre, m
widow -- viuda, f
widower -- viudo, m
width -- anchura, f
  (w. of cloth) ancho
wig -- (hair) cabellera
wild -- salvaje; ladino, m
William -- Guillermo
win -- ganar; vencer
wind -- viento aire
wind -- (w. a watch)
  dar cueda
windmill -- papalote, m
windshield -- parabrisa,
  m
window -- ventana, f;
  ventanilla
    (casement w.)
    ventana, f
    (small w.)
    ventanilla, f
    (w. pane) vidrio
    (w. sill) repisa de
    la ventana
windpipe -- traquea, f
wine -- vino, m
    (w. bottle) botella
    de vino

(w. glass) vaso
  (para vino)
(w. cup) copa (para
  vino)
(red w.) vino tinto
(port w.) vino de
  Oporto
winter -- invierno, m
wipe -- limpiar
  (rub) frotar
  (dry) secar
wire -- alambre, m
  (barbed w.) alambre
  de pico
  (net w.) alambre de
  tela
  (slick w.) alambre
  liso
  (w. cutters) corta
  de alambres, m
wise -- sabio; docto;
  erudito
wish -- querer; desear
wishbone -- espoleta, f
with -- con; en companía
  de
within -- dentro de
without -- fuera; sin;
  afuera
wolf -- lobo, m
woman -- mujer, f
wood -- madera, f
wood -- (fire) leña, f

161

wood chopper -- lenador, m
woods -- bosque, m; monte, m
woodwork -- (in house) maderaje
wool -- lana, f
word -- palabra, f
workman -- obrero,
work -- trabajar; obrar; trabajo, m; empleo, m; obra, f
worker -- trabajador, m; jornalero, m
workshop -- taller, m
world -- mundo, m
worms -- (cut w.) troncidores, m (screw w.) gusanos, m
worry -- afligir; apurarse
worse -- peor
worst -- el peor; la peor, etc.
wound -- herida, f
wrap -- envolver
wrapping paper -- papel de envolver
wreck -- choque, m; chocar
wrench -- llave, f
wrinkle -- arruga, f

wrist -- muñeca, f; pulsera, f
write -- escribir
writing desk -- escritorio
wrong -- incorrecto; falso, m

X

x-rays -- rayos

Y

yams -- camote
yard -- (at house) jardín (measure) yarda; vara, f
yarn -- hilaza, f; hilo, m
New Year's Day -- día de año nuevo
year -- año, m (last y.) el año pasado (next y.) el año próximo
yeast -- levadura, f
yell -- gritar
yellow -- amarillo
yes -- sí
yesterday -- ayer
yet -- todavía
yolk -- (of egg) yema, f
yonder -- allá
you -- usted; ustedes (polite)

you -- tu; vosotros (as)
(familiar)
young -- joven
younger -- menor
youngest -- el menor, etc.
young lady -- señorita, f
your -- su
yours -- el suyo, etc.

Z

zebra -- cebra, f
zero -- zero; cero, m
zinc -- zinc, cina, m
zinc oxide -- óxido de
cinc, m
zone -- banda; faja, f;
zona
zoo -- jardín zoológico